GEORGE S. PATTON

LEADERSHIP ▪ STRATEGY ▪ CONFLICT

STEVEN J. ZALOGA

First published in Great Britain in 2010 by Osprey Publishing,
Midland House, West Way, Botley, Oxford OX2 0PH, UK
44-02 23rd St, Suite 219, Long Island City, NY 11101, USA

E-mail: info@ospreypublishing.com

© 2010 Osprey Publishing Ltd

All rights reserved. Apart from any fair dealing for the purpose of private
study, research, criticism or review, as permitted under the Copyright,
Designs and Patents Act, 1988, no part of this publication may be
reproduced, stored in a retrieval system, or transmitted in any form
or by any means, electronic, electrical, chemical, mechanical, optical,
photocopying, recording or otherwise, without the prior written permission
of the copyright owner. Enquiries should be addressed to the Publishers.

A CIP catalogue record for this book is available from the British Library.

ISBN: 978 1 84603 459 6
E-book ISBN: 978 1 84908 283 9

Editorial by Ilios Publishing Ltd, Oxford, UK (www.iliospublishing.com)
Page layout by Myriam Bell Design, France
Index by Mike Parkin
Typeset in Stone Serif and Officina Sans
Maps by Mapping Specialists Ltd
Originated by PDQ Media, Bungay, Suffolk
Printed in China through Worldprint Ltd

10 11 12 13 14   10 9 8 7 6 5 4 3 2 1

Author's note

The author would like to thank the Patton Museum at Ft. Knox,
Kentucky, for their generous help, especially Candace Fuller of the
museum's splendid library and research center. A nod of appreciation
also goes to the staffs of the US Army Military History Institute at
Carlisle Barracks, Pennsylvania, and the National Archives and Records
Administration (NARA) at College Park, Maryland.

Artist's note

Readers may care to note that the original paintings from which the
colour plates in this book were prepared are available for private sale.
The Publishers retain all reproduction copyright whatsoever.
All enquiries should be addressed to:

Steve Noon, 50 Colchester Avenue, Penylan, Cardiff, CF23 9BP, UK

The Publishers regret that they can enter into no correspondence upon
this matter.

US Army unit numbering

This book follows the US Army's standard World War II practice in the
numbering of tactical formations: Arabic numerals for army groups
(for example, 12th Army Group), spelled numbers for field armies
(for example, Third Army), Roman numerals for corps (for example,
XX Corps) and Arabic numerals for divisions (for example,
4th Armored Division).

The Woodland Trust

Osprey Publishing are supporting the Woodland Trust, the UK's leading
woodland conservation charity, by funding the dedication of trees.

FOR A CATALOGUE OF ALL BOOKS PUBLISHED BY OSPREY
MILITARY AND AVIATION PLEASE CONTACT:

Osprey Direct, c/o Random House Distribution Center,
400 Hahn Road, Westminster, MD 21157
Email: uscustomerservice@ospreypublishing.com

Osprey Direct, The Book Service Ltd, Distribution Centre, Colchester Road, Frating Green, Colchester, Essex, CO7 7DW
E-mail: customerservice@ospreypublishing.com

www.ospreypublishing.com

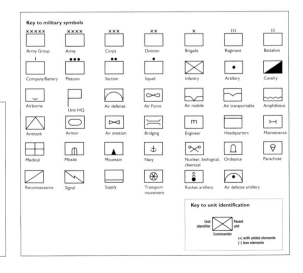

CONTENTS

INTRODUCTION

Courtney Hodges, Alexander Patch, William Simpson, Ray Porter, Robert Eichelberger. Recognize any of these generals? Probably not, unless you are a particularly well-informed military history reader. These were George S. Patton's contemporaries in World War II, but today their names are almost forgotten.

George S. Patton Jr. is among the most recognized American commanders of all time. Patton began his career in the cavalry and played a celebrated but minor role in the punitive mission against Pancho Villa in Mexico in 1916. During World War I, Patton trained and led the first US Army tank battalions, but was wounded in his second battle during the Meuse-Argonne offensive. Patton's legend began to emerge in the run up to World War II. His dramatic and heroic persona stood in stark contrast to the staid, managerial style of most US Army commanders and he attracted public attention even before Pearl Harbor in 1941. He led the Western Task Force landings in French North Africa in November 1942 as part of Operation *Torch*, but his most important mission was as a diplomat to coax the Vichy French army into the Allied fold. Patton redeemed the honor of the US Army after the Kasserine Pass debacle in Tunisia in 1943 with its first tactical victory against the Wehrmacht at El Guettar in March 1943. When British planners managed to sideline his Seventh Army during operations on Sicily in July 1943, Patton's aggressive determination pushed the US units to Palermo, setting the stage for the concluding capture of Messina after Montgomery's advance bogged down. Patton's fortunes ebbed in late 1943 as the result of his rash behavior when he slapped two shell-shocked soldiers. Yet Eisenhower knew he needed a bold armor commander for the operations in France, and so shielded Patton from further recriminations. Ike's foresight saved Patton for his most important contributions in the European Theater of Operations (ETO) in 1944 and 1945.

Patton was assigned command of the Third Army that formed the second wave of American field armies committed to France. The Third Army was first deployed in the wake of Operation *Cobra* in late July 1944, the breakout from Normandy. Although Patton was assigned the secondary role of liberating Brittany, he saw the futility of this mission and argued with Bradley and

Eisenhower that there was a fleeting opportunity to exploit German weakness and conduct a bold race to the Seine. Against crumbling German opposition, Patton was at the doorstep of Paris in less than two weeks, completely undermining Wehrmacht attempts to reconstitute a defensive line in France after their defeat in Normandy. Advancing toward the traditional gateway into Germany via the Nancy corridor in Lorraine, Patton was frustrated in the autumn of 1944 when a shortage of supplies and inclement weather halted the Third Army at the great fortress city of Metz. The Third Army was ready to resume the offensive into Germany in mid-December when the Wehrmacht struck in the Ardennes. With his forces already poised for action, Patton promoted a bold plan to strike the Germans in the flank and relieve the trapped garrison in Bastogne. Patton helped reverse the German offensive, and his Third Army was the US Army's fire brigade

An official army portrait of Lieutenant-General George S. Patton Jr., commander of Third Army, following his promotion to full general with his fourth star on April 17, 1945. (NARA)

once again, racing to the rescue when the situation seemed hopeless. When given a secondary role again in the February offensives into Germany, Patton captured attention with a bold armored attack that pushed through German defenses in the Saar and Palatinate. While Montgomery prepared an elephantine Rhine crossing further north, Patton's Third Army leapt the Rhine on the run near Mainz relying on speed and shock rather than brute force. The momentum of Patton's Third Army was so great that after Eisenhower ordered most US units to halt along the Elbe in late April 1945, Patton was given the mission of continuing into Czechoslovakia and Austria to rout any Nazi last-ditch defenders. Patton's Third Army had advanced further, captured more enemy prisoners and liberated more territory than any other Allied field army in the ETO. After many brushes with death, Patton died in an auto accident in December 1945.

Patton, more than any other Allied field army commander, demonstrated the offensive shock power of modern mechanized forces when exercised with a cavalryman's boldness. He was the *enfant terrible* of the US Army in the ETO whose accomplishments sometimes were tarnished by his rash and impetuous behavior. Patton's legend was burned into American popular culture with the 1970 release of the award-winning film *Patton*.

THE EARLY YEARS

George Smith Patton was the third in his family to bear the name. His family traced its lineage back to Robert Paton (later Patton) who departed Scotland in 1770 and settled in Virginia, becoming a prosperous businessman. The first George Smith Patton, born in 1833, attended the Virginia Military Institute (VMI). He helped form the Kanawha Rifleman, a militia that took part in one of the opening moves of the Civil War, mobilizing to repulse John Brown's insurrection at Harper's Ferry in 1859. Of the nine boys in his family, seven served in the Confederate Army during the Civil War and two were killed in action. George S. Patton was wounded early in the war during a skirmish at Scary Creek in July 1861, but recovered and took command of the 22nd Virginia Infantry. He was wounded again in May 1862 at the battle of Giles Courthouse. Patton's younger brother, Waller Tazewell Patton, was killed leading the 7th Virginia Infantry during Pickett's charge, part of the battle of Gettysburg in July 1863. The family legend was solidly established at the battle of New Market on May 15, 1864, when George S. Patton's 22nd Virginia Infantry reinforced the valiant VMI Corps of Cadets in the legendary Confederate victory; several other Pattons fought in the battle. Colonel Patton was mortally wounded at the age of 31 during the fighting near Winchester on September 19, 1864, while leading the Patton Brigade against Major-General Philip Sheridan's cavalry.

Patton's young son, George William Patton, changed his name to George Smith Patton II in 1868 to honor his father's memory. The Patton family was destitute in the wake of the Civil War, but family members in California convinced Susan Patton and her family to leave their beloved Virginia and establish a new life in the West. Young George S. Patton II returned to Virginia in 1871 to attend VMI, graduating with distinction in 1877 but he forsook a military career to address the family's lingering financial problems, becoming a successful lawyer. In December 1884, he married Ruth Wilson, the daughter of Benjamin "Don Benito" Wilson, one of the pioneers of southern California. The Wilson connection restored the family of George S. Patton II as prosperous landowners.

George Smith Patton Jr. was born on November 11, 1885. He lived a comfortable childhood amongst the extended Patton and Wilson families on the Lake Vineyard estate, a spoiled and pampered son of a wealthy land-owning family. Patton's upbringing helped create his passion for a military career. His father's hopes to follow in the heroic footsteps of the original Col. Patton were frustrated by family needs, and so dreams of glory and the sword were passed on to his son. "Georgie" was regaled with tales of the family's martial glory in the Civil War, and readings from the *Iliad* and *Odyssey* were a staple fare even at a young age. His doting aunt Nannie took over much of his early education, and readings from the Bible and the classics predominated. Patton's early heroes were the Confederate Civil War generals, but also the legends of literature and antiquity: Siegfried, Beowulf, Xenophon, Alexander the Great and Napoleon. But above all, his father inculcated in young Georgie the belief that the Pattons came from special stock, with a noble military tradition and a special responsibility of service. Patton learned to ride horses on the same saddle on which his grandfather and namesake had been mortally wounded at Winchester. Georgie's favorite toys were swords, and his father gave him two horses of his own when he reached the age of ten; his destiny in the cavalry seemed preordained. If his upbringing was unusually slanted towards ancestor worship and military glory, it was also profoundly religious. The Pattons had long been stalwarts of the Episcopalian Church, and Patton later recalled that as a child he prayed ardently to the Lord not to give him the call to religious service in the clergy since he so much wanted to become a soldier.

George S. Patton Jr. did not begin formal schooling until the age of 11. The noted historian Carlo D'Este in his biography contends that young Patton suffered from a learning disorder, dyslexia. Dyslexics have difficulties with visual expressions of language and mathematics, such as reading and writing, though they cope normally with the spoken language. Patton had no difficulties in remembering vast passages of the Bible or literary accounts. In spite of their intelligence, dyslexics consider themselves stupid and feel compelled to prove themselves to others. In some cases this leads to boasting, but often to an overwhelming need to achieve. Even when dyslexics succeed, they sometimes feel that they have been lucky or merely fooled others, further fueling their need to achieve. Some prominent dyslexics in Patton's time were Albert Einstein, Thomas Edison, and President Woodrow Wilson. Dyslexia may have been at the root of many of Patton's problems in his early career; if so it was also a catalyst for his eventual successes, contributing both to his persistence and ambition. The issue of Patton's dyslexia and its effects on his early career remain a subject of some controversy amongst his biographers.

The Pattons had strong ties to VMI, but recognized that the US Military Academy at West Point was a more secure route to success. George S. Patton Jr. spent a year at VMI in preparation for West Point and his father's political influence helped secure the necessary Congressional appointment. He entered West Point in 1904 and faced daunting challenges due to his academic difficulties. He did poorly at team sports, such as football, but became a star at track and field and fencing. He failed mathematics in his freshman year, and so was turned back a year. The setback proved temporary and the repeated year saw Patton gain more self-assurance and master many of his academic difficulties. He was comfortable with the trappings of military life, always in proper uniform and with impeccable military posture. He stood out as a particularly determined cadet, even if his academic performance remained mediocre.

Patton in uniform after returning from France in 1919, a young captain facing uncertain prospects in a greatly diminished peacetime army. (Patton Museum)

He was never a popular member of the class, his naked ambition alienating most other classmates. Curiously enough, this class included all three future commanders of the armies of Bradley's 12th Army Group: Patton of the Third Army, William Simpson of the Ninth and Courtney Hodges of the First Army. (Hodges dropped out of the class for academic reasons and rose through the ranks.) Patton's other classmate's included several other prominent World War II leaders including Bradley's counterpart, Jacob Devers, who led the 6th Army Group, Robert Eichelberger, who led the Eight Army in the Pacific, and the controversial J. C. Lee who commanded US Army rear services in the ETO.

During his years at West Point, Patton had courted Beatrice Ayer, daughter of the self-made millionaire Frederich Ayer of Boston. Ayer was not pleased with the idea of a son-in-law in the hardscrabble turn-of-the-century army, a career viewed by most prominent Americans as a backwater of losers and ne'er-do-wells. But Ayers was friendly with the Patton family and finally consented to the marriage in 1910.

THE MILITARY LIFE

Lieutenant-Colonel George S. Patton, commander of the 1st/304th Tank Brigade, standing in front of one of his Renault FT light tanks at the Bourg tank school on July 15, 1918. (NARA)

Patton's choice of the cavalry was inevitable, and in 1909 he was assigned to Ft. Sheridan, Illinois. The assignment was short lived, as Patton was able to use family connections to be reassigned to Ft. Myer, Virginia, the army's most prestigious cavalry post. It was residence of the army chief-of-staff and placed the ambitious young Patton in the midst of the social and political life of Washington, DC. Patton made the most of the opportunities, striking up a friendship with Secretary of War Henry Stimson after a chance encounter on one of the post's equestrian trails. In 1912, Patton became the first army officer to represent the United States at a new pentathlon event at the Fifth Olympiad in Stockholm, finishing a very respectable fifth in the competition. An offshoot of the Olympics was a brief course in swordsmanship with Adjutant M. Cléry, master of arms and fencing instructor at France's legendary Saumur cavalry school. The wealth of the Patton and Ayers families helped lubricate Patton's expensive lifestyle at Ft. Myer, funding an automobile and a stable of horses for his polo playing. He rubbed shoulders with the army chief-of-staff, Major-General Leonard

Wood, on the equestrian trails and Patton became an aide to Wood at the War Department in late 1912. Patton assisted in the Ordnance design of the M1913 saber, popularly called the Patton sword. With the ear of Simpson and Wood, in June 1913 the army granted Patton authorization to attend the Saumur cavalry school at his own expense to further study swordsmanship. Patton used the opportunity in the summer of 1913 to travel by auto with his wife and infant daughter from the port of Cherbourg through Normandy's bocage country to Saumur in the Loire valley. It was his first contact with the terrain where he would secure his great victories three decades later. On return from France, Patton was assigned to Ft. Riley, Kansas, home of the army's Mounted Service School. As an acknowledged "Master of the Sword," Patton was in the unique position of being both a student at the school and an instructor.

Patton can be seen here with his back to the camera amongst the instructors at the Bourg tank school inspecting a group of tankers and their Renault FT tanks on July 15, 1918. The officer to Patton's immediate left is Captain Ranulf Compton, his chief instructor. (NARA)

In 1915, Patton was on the verge of being transferred to the Philippines, a potential disaster to his ambitions. War was raging in Europe, and Patton rightly believed that a tour at a distant colonial outpost would ensure his obscurity. His tour at Ft. Myer served him well, and he was able to get reassigned to the 8th Cavalry Regiment at Ft. Bliss, Texas, on the Mexican border. It was another fortuitous decision. Tensions with Mexico were rising as the civil war there spilled over the American frontier. Brigadier-General John "Black Jack" Pershing was sent to Ft. Bliss to take control of US forces along the border. Patton's troop was dispatched to garrison Sierra Blanca, a violent cowboy town every bit as rough as any Old West legend. Patton's attempt to emulate the local gunfighters by wearing his Colt .45 automatic in his belt instead of a holster nearly ended in tragedy when it accidently discharged one night in a saloon. Although he escaped wounding himself in the incident, Patton gave up the automatic for an old-fashioned, ivory-handled Colt 1873 revolver in a holster, a weapon that would become his signature in years to come.

Patton eventually returned to a more domestic setting at Ft. Bliss with his wife and young family. His sister Nita visited and became involved in a short-lived love affair with the recently widowed Black Jack Pershing that might have resulted in marriage had World War I not intervened. The troubles along the Mexican border intensified in early 1916 when Pancho Villa began his raids into New Mexico in revenge for US political support of his rival. Pershing was ordered to stage a punitive expedition into Mexico, and Patton was chagrined to learn his troop of the 8th Cavalry Regiment would not participate. Patton rudely skirted official channels and directly approached Pershing about obtaining a post on the expedition. Pershing

had himself played the same stunt in 1898 to participate in the Spanish-American War, and consented to Patton becoming one of his aides.

Pershing's frequent contacts with Patton at headquarters saw him impressed with the young officer's eagerness and bravery. Patton came to wider attention on May 14, 1916, during his first brush with combat. The Pershing force had been attempting to capture the commander of Villa's *Dorades* bodyguards, "General" Julio Cárdenas. An earlier large-scale raid on his uncle's San Miguelito ranch had failed to turn him up, but during a foraging expedition,

When Congress abolished the Tank Corps, Patton chose to return to his military roots in the cavalry in spite of the unpromising prospects of the branch in modern warfare. Although viewed as one of America's top tank experts, Patton realized that that his military career would be derailed if he acted as a lonely prophet of mechanization. (Patton Museum)

Patton decided to stage a small surprise raid on the ranch. Patton's force included ten soldiers from the 6th Infantry Regiment and two civilian guides moving fast in three Dodge touring cars. The cars raced across low ground, approaching the ranch unnoticed, and burst over a rise a short distance from the main house. The three cars pulled to a halt outside the ranch, and the troops poured out to trap any armed Mexicans inside. Three riders emerged on horses through one of the gates of the hacienda, and were brought under fire by Patton and the other soldiers. In a chaotic gun battle, all three Mexicans were brought down, one of them Cárdenas. The punitive expedition to that point had been an exercise in frustration, so the press pounced on the incident. Patton was celebrated as the "bandit killer," even though it was not clear whether Patton had hit or killed any of Villa's men. Regardless of his personal marksmanship, Patton's bravery and initiative had been at the core of the successful raid and did not go unnoticed by Pershing. Patton received his promotion to first lieutenant shortly afterwards on May 23, 1916. The more important consequence for Patton would come a year later when the United States was drawn into the European war. Pershing was assigned to command the American Expeditionary Force (AEF) and Patton had little trouble in receiving an assignment on Pershing's staff.

After a frustrating spell at Pershing's headquarters at Chaumont, Patton craved combat action. A sympathetic staff officer told Patton that "we want to start a tank school and to get anything out of tanks one must be reckless and take risks. I think you are the sort of darned fool who will do it." On November 10, 1917, he was dispatched to establish the AEF Light Tank School. Patton received a quick orientation from the French on the new Renault FT light tank while on November 20, 1917, the British launched their attack on Cambrai, the first successful use of massed tanks in the war. Patton visited British tank expert Colonel J. F. C. Fuller to learn the lessons of Cambrai, and quickly established himself as the AEF's expert on the new weapon. He was a demanding and energetic leader, and the obvious choice to lead the first two tank battalions into combat. He became a lieutenant-colonel in early April 1918, a heady rise from being a lieutenant a year before. As training continued at Bourg, Patton attended the General Staff School at Langres where he rubbed shoulders with many of the up-and-coming officers who would be leaders in a subsequent war: George C. Marshall, army chief-of-staff in World War II, was among his instructors. Patton's brigade was finally committed to action during the St. Mihiel offensive in September 1918, at one point supporting Brigadier-General Douglas MacArthur's 84th Infantry Brigade. On September 26, Patton's tanks were again in action during the Meuse-Argonne offensive. When the attack stalled in a German trench line, Patton made his way forward to prod his unit forward. Of the seven men who accompanied Patton forward, five were killed and he suffered a severe wound in the upper left thigh; his batman pulled him to safety and he was later awarded the Distinguished Service Cross for his actions. It was a difficult recuperation and Patton lost 30lb in the process. He returned to command the tank school as a full colonel, but his wound kept him from further combat duty.

On returning to the United States after the war, Patton was assigned to the new Tank Corps center at Camp Meade, Maryland. His new neighbor at Camp Meade in 1919 was Lieutenant-Colonel Dwight Eisenhower who had led the tank training center at Camp Colt, Pennsylvania, during the war. Eisenhower was five years younger than Patton, West Point class of 1915, but both were ardent supporters of the tank and students of military doctrine. The friendship established at Camp Meade would have critical consequences two decades later. The US Army was rapidly demobilized after the war and trimmed back to a skeleton force. The Tank Corps was disbanded and absorbed into the infantry; Patton chose to return to the cavalry and was assigned to Ft. Myer and the 3rd Cavalry Regiment as a major. In 1923, he attended the Command and General Staff College at Ft. Leavenworth, Kansas, an essential hurdle to high command. Patton served another tour of duty in Washington in the late 1920s and attended the Army War College starting in 1931. The interwar years were frustrating for Patton. One of his efficiency reports duly noted that he was "better qualified for active duty than the routine of office work." He was never a maverick, and in spite of his reputation as the army's foremost tank expert, he gave up any visionary role in the mechanization debate, realizing the

Patton's dynamic performance during the 1941 wargames kept him in consideration for advancement in spite of his age. Here, the "Green Hornet" is seen in his command half-track in Manchester, Tennessee, on June 19, 1941, wearing the experimental plastic Riddell football helmet he proposed as the new headgear for the Armored Force. One of his staff officers, Lieutenant-Colonel Robert Grow, is trying to gather some impromptu intelligence from a local citizen. Grow would later serve as commander of the 6th Armored Division, one of two armored divisions almost continuously under Patton's Third Army in the 1944–45 campaigns in the ETO. (NARA)

Patton overlooks the progress of a pontoon bridge over the Red River on September 8, 1941, during the Third Army wargames in Louisiana. These helped impress on Patton the vital necessity of tactical bridging as a prerequisite for mobility in warfare. (NARA)

harm it would do to his career in the very conservative cavalry branch. In one of his most disagreeable acts while in uniform, Patton led the 3rd Cavalry Regiment in dispersing the AEF veterans of the "Bonus Army" protests in Washington in July 1932; among the protestors was Joe Angelo, his batman in 1918, who had saved his life when he was wounded. He suffered bouts of depression, endured more injuries from riding accidents, and his marriage suffered growing strains.

September 1939 saw Patton again at Ft. Myer with the new army chief-of-staff, George C. Marshall, temporarily sharing the Patton quarters. With war enveloping Europe, Marshall was updating his legendary "black book" of names of promising officers who would be needed to rebuild America's pathetic peacetime army. Patton was a rare case of an officer over 55 still earmarked by Marshall due to his talents and vigor. Marshall bluntly noted: "George will take a unit through hell and high water... but keep a tight rope around his neck... give him an armored corps when one becomes available." The spring maneuvers of 1940 and the defeat of France in May–June 1940 convinced Patton that the days of his beloved horse cavalry were over. Though Patton had been unwilling to promote the tank during the lean years of the 1930s, another cavalry maverick, Adna

Baptism of fire: St. Mihiel, September 12, 1918

Patton's two tank battalions were committed to action in the St. Mihiel salient in support of the 42nd Rainbow Division. Patton was instructed by his commander, Gen. Samuel Rockenbach, to remain at the brigade headquarters and to stay in touch by radio. However, communication with the advancing tanks was virtually impossible and by mid-morning, Patton left his adjutant in charge of the headquarters and headed into the field to determine the progress of his advancing tanks. The rainy season had already begun and the ground was "sticky, soggy, awful mud in which the tanks wallowed belly deep." Although Patton had shown the foresight to have the tanks carry extra drums of fuel, the soggy soil soon exhausted their fuel supply and many tanks were left behind out of gas or stuck in the mud. Here, Patton is seen consulting with one of his tank company commanders from the 344th Tank Battalion in the afternoon after the attack had run out of steam. Patton later wrote: "General Rockenbach gave me hell for going up but it had to be done. At least I will not sit in a dug-out and have my men out fighting." Patton would pay the price for his aggressiveness a few weeks later on September 26 when he was severely wounded while checking on his tanks' progress during the Meuse-Argonne offensive.

Chaffee, had been willing to buck the trend. So when the Armored Force was formed in July 1940, it was Chaffee who took command. With the expanding army in dire need of talent, Patton was given his first star and a brigade command in the newly formed 2nd Armored Division at Ft. Benning, Georgia, in July 1940. The prospect of another war rejuvenated Patton from his depression and doldrums of the 1930s. Patton's energy and training skills helped create the new division; after the laxity of the peacetime years, he became notorious for his high standards of discipline and military dress. Divisional command of the 2nd Armored Division soon followed, and Patton led the division during the November 1941 wargames in the Carolinas, winning accolades for his leadership. His superior performance during the exercises convinced Marshall to earmark him for one of the army's senior combat commands.

Patton strikes a pose shooting an azimuth with his lensatic compass while standing in front of his M3 light tank at the Desert Training Center in the Mojave Desert of California in 1942. He is again seen wearing one of the experimental Riddell plastic football helmets. Note also that he is armed with a .22-cal. Woodsman target pistol in a special holster, not his trademark ivory-handled Colt .45-cal. Peacemaker revolvers. (NARA)

It was around this time that Patton began to acquire several of his nicknames. He proposed a new green uniform for the tank crews including a football helmet; this combined with his fondness for charging around base on a command car with sirens blazing prompted the soldiers to refer to him as the "Green Hornet" after the popular comic-book character. Patton was also legendary for his profane and lurid pep talks to the men, and he became known as "blood and guts" from one of his much-used expressions. He attracted national attention when his photo appeared on the cover of *Life* magazine highlighting his recent exploits.

Shortly after America was dragged into the war in December 1941, Patton was again promoted to lead I Armored Corps at Ft. Benning. Patton was convinced that the US Army would eventually become involved in the war in the North African desert, and was among the advocates for a more realistic training ground in the wastes of the Mojave Desert in southern California. The Desert Training Center was created by Patton in March 1942 and would again demonstrate Patton's often-overlooked importance in training US troops. The assignment was short lived as in July he was ordered to Washington where he was assigned to command the Western Task Force in Operation *Torch*, the amphibious landing near Casablanca.

Patton's assignment to lead an element of the North African command was due both to Marshall's assessment of him after the Carolina wargames, as well as his long-standing friendship with Dwight Eisenhower, who had become Marshall's right-hand man. In turn, Patton began to assemble around him a command staff that would stay with him for most of the war. These were officers he had known during the bleak 1930s – Geoffrey Keyes who became his deputy; Hobart Gay his chief-of-staff; Kent Lambert his operations officer (G-3) and Walter Muller, his logistician (G-4). There would be some changes to his staff in later years. Among the most important additions was Oscar Koch, who was arguably the best intelligence officer (G-2) in Europe, and Hugh Gaffey would become his deputy after Keyes assumed corps command after Sicily. Patton's ability to command in the field depended on the skills of these officers to execute his orders, and Patton eventually created one of the best staffs in the US Army. This is a point of some controversy as both Bradley and Hodge's staffs would impugn the quality of Patton's staff after the war. Arguably, the proof can be measured by performance, and Patton's staff certainly stood the measure compared to the performance of rival field army staffs.

Back to war. Patton poses for a portrait on board the cruiser USS *Augusta* while on the way to North Africa and Operation *Torch* in November 1942. (NARA)

THE HOUR OF DESTINY

North Africa 1942–43

Patton's Western Task Force landed on November 9, 1942, one of three US forces landing in Morocco and Algeria to catch Rommel's Afrika Korps in a vise with Montgomery's Eighth Army attacking from the east. The fighting

One of Patton's most important contributions to the Allied cause in North Africa was his successful diplomacy to convert the French forces from opponent to ally. He is seen here with the military governor of Morocco, Général Auguste Paul Noguès, during a review of French troops on December 18, 1942.

around Casablanca was one of the most peculiar skirmishes in Patton's career. The United States wanted to seize the Vichy France colonies without antagonizing the French Army of Africa since there were hopes that they might switch sides and join the Allies. This indeed occurred after a few days of desultory combat, with the French fighting long enough to satisfy military honor. There was little sympathy in the French Army for the Axis, and senior French commanders deemed extended resistance pointless. Patton's role after the Casablanca fighting was to oversee the garrisoning of Morocco as a counterweight to any possible German reinforcement of North Africa via Spain or southern France. His role was more diplomatic than military, and he carried it off with considerable grace and aplomb. His affection for the French Army since his days at Saumur and his considerable charm were significant assets for what might have been a troubled start to the rejuvenation of the French Army. Patton's diplomatic abilities were an often-overlooked aspect of his military career, and one shown to best effect in French North Africa.

Patton and his staff pose for a group portrait. From left to right, Colonel Hobart "Hap" Gay, Patton, Colonel Kent Lambert, Major-General Geoffrey Keyes, and Captain Richard Jenson. (NARA)

The fortunes of Major-General's Lloyd Fredendall's II Corps in neighboring Tunisia saw a steep decline after Hitler dispatched General der Panzertrupe Hans-Jürgen von Arnim's 5. Panzerarmee to reinforce Rommel. The American corps was woefully overextended and Rommel saw this as an opportunity to redeem his faltering reputation with a sudden attack toward Kasserine Pass in February 1943. The poor performance of the US Army in their combat

Patton takes Palermo, July 22 1943

Patton was incensed that his Seventh US Army was allotted a secondary role in protecting the flank of Montgomery's Eighth British Army on Sicily, and so engineered his own mission to race for Palermo on the northern coast. His deputy, Maj. Gen. Geoffrey Keyes, was assigned to lead a provisional corps that included the 3rd Infantry Division, 82nd Airborne Division and 2nd Armored Division. The advance began on July 19, 1943, with spearheads from Darby's Rangers. The 100-mile (160km) advance through the mountains faced little opposition, and American units congregated outside the city on July 22. The city's defense was in the hands of an ad hoc formation, called Post Defense N made up of Italian coastal defense units. The Italian commander, Gen. Giovanni Marciani, was captured by the 82nd Reconnaissance Battalion. The surrender of the garrison was formally accepted at 1900hrs on July 22 by Maj. Gen. Keyes. Patton (1) arrived around 2100hrs. He is seen here the next day visiting one of the city's landmarks, the Cattedrale di Palermo. In the background, the 2nd Armored Division commander, Maj. Gen. Ernie Harmon (2) chats with Patton's chief of staff, Brig. Gen. Hap Gay (3). Behind them is Keyes' modified M3A1 scout car (4).

debut led to a crisis in the American command in North Africa, and Eisenhower chose Patton to redeem II Corps. Patton responded in his trademark fashion with a flurry of activity. Textbook discipline was imposed, training was stepped up, and "Georgie" showed up everywhere, prodding officers and cajoling the troops with his impromptu pep talks. Symptomatic of his changes was an instruction that officers would henceforth stop the practice of hiding their rank insignia for fear it would attract snipers. "That's part of your job being an officer" he scolded them. When leading their men into battle they were as expendable and would have to take the same risks as the lowliest private. For all of his hard-hearted bluster, Patton was devastated by the death of his aide, Dick Jenson, who was killed during a Luftwaffe raid in Tunisia while undertaking an assignment for him.

British senior commanders were skeptical of the fighting abilities of their newly arrived Allies, and Patton was insistent that II Corps be committed to the final campaign in Tunisia to prove it had become battleworthy. On March 23, the 10. Panzer-Division made a clumsy attack into the advancing 1st Infantry Division near El Guettar and received a very bloody nose in the process. The skirmish was not especially important in military terms, but it helped restore the confidence of II Corps and established Patton's reputation as a "fighting general." Rommel later wrote:

The two candidates to replace the failed Fredendall after Kasserine Pass were Patton and Major-General Ernie Harmon. Harmon (left) had been assigned by Eisenhower to report on II Corps' problems and recommended relieving Fredendall, so he thought it inappropriate to replace him. (NARA)

Ike pins on a third star as Patton was elevated to lieutenant-general while visiting his headquarters on March 13, 1943, following his assumption of command of II Corps in the wake of Kasserine Pass. (NARA)

Top: The US victory over the 10. Panzer-Division at El Guettar in March 1943 helped restore American confidence after the Kasserine debacle. This photo taken during the fighting shows Patton with the 1st Infantry Division "Big Red One" division commanders, Major-General "Terrible Terry" Allen in the center and his deputy, Brigadier-General Theodore Roosevelt, one of President Teddy Roosevelt's sons, on the left. The performance of the 1st Infantry Division at El Guettar led Patton to insist on a change of plan for the Sicily landings, with 1st Infantry Division assigned to the critical Gela sector instead of a green division. It was a fortuitous change in view of the 1st Infantry Division's splendid performance in the face of a Panzer counterattack. (NARA)

Bottom: Patton sits on a hill, overlooking the battle of El Guettar as it unfolds below on March 23, 1943. This well-known photograph was staged by the Signal Corps, embodying the romantic and heroic image that Patton wished to project. (NARA)

In Tunisia, the Americans had to pay a stiff price for their experience, but it brought them rich dividends. Even at that time, the American generals showed themselves to be very advanced in their tactical handling of their forces, although we had to wait until the Patton army in France to see their most astonishing achievements in mobile warfare. The Americans, it is fair to say, profited far more than the British from their experience in Africa, thus confirming the axiom that education is easier than re-education.

While in command of I Armored Corps in Tunisia in the winter of 1942–43, Patton had an M3A1 scout car modified for his use with additional armor shields on the front and rear. He continued to use it while commanding II Corps in Tunisia and is seen here south of Gafsa on March 30, 1943. (NARA)

Tunisia exacerbated Anglo-American tensions at the senior command level. The British Army commanders deemed the US Army insufficiently prepared and not yet battleworthy. Although Eisenhower retained overall command, all senior command slots in the Mediterranean theater went to British officers. The senior US Army commanders recognized that their forces were inexperienced but also blamed poor British deployment decisions for the initial troubles at Kasserine. In contrast to US attitudes towards the Royal Navy and RAF, the US Army had a jaundiced view of the performance of the British Army in the desert war and little confidence in their advice. Eisenhower put a lid on US complaints and made it clear that any officer impugning the British Army would have his career abruptly ended. The angry stew of British condescension and American resentment soured command relations.

Sicily: July 1943

Once the situation in Tunisia improved, Eisenhower recalled Patton in April to take over control of plans for the American side of Operation *Husky*, the Allied invasion of Sicily scheduled for July 1943. Patton was given another star, and, as a lieutenant-general, was put in command of the Seventh Army. His deputy in Tunisia, Omar Bradley, commanded one of the two corps assigned to the mission. Patton was growing increasingly weary of British dominance in the planning process, and was incensed that his Seventh Army would do little more on Sicily than act as a flank guard for Montgomery's Eighth Army.

The landings on Sicily on July 10 encountered fierce resistance in the American sector with a Panzer counteroffensive against the 1st Infantry Division lodgment near Gela. Alexander's diffident direction of the campaign left the initiative to his strong-willed commanders. Montgomery was content to leave Patton's Seventh Army in the secondary role of flank security and his decision to swing west into the sector previously assigned to Patton's 45th Infantry Division aggravated relations without benefit to the campaign. Patton decided that he needed to take matters into his own hands, and began to engineer a mission for the Seventh Army, the capture of the Sicilian capital of Palermo on the northwest coast. With Montgomery's advance stalled, Alexander acceded to Patton's scheme. Geoffrey Keyes, Patton's deputy, led a provisional corps that reached Palermo on July 23. It is unclear if he had planned to do so from the start, but once in Palermo, Patton began eyeing a race to Messina along the north coast. While considerable fodder has been made of antagonisms between Montgomery and Patton, this was not one of them. Patton's ambitious scheme was not directed against Montgomery so much as it was at redeeming the reputation of the US Army and establishing his own reputation in the process. The terrain and fierce German resistance had stymied Montgomery's advance to Messina, and he was professional enough to see the merit in Patton's audacious scheme. Patton's troops reached Messina on August 17 with a series of bold amphibious leapfrogs up the northwest coast.

Patton's dramatic successes on Sicily put him in the premier position for further major commands in the forthcoming European campaign. But his theatrical excesses and temper nearly brought his military career to an end. Unlike many other American commanders, Patton frequently visited combat

Previous page: Patton's lieutenants for the forthcoming Operation *Husky* on Sicily are seen here in June 1943. From left to right they are Major-General Ernie Harmon (2nd Armored Division); Major-General Manton Eddy (9th Infantry Division); Major-General Omar Bradley (II Corps); Major-General Charles Ryder (34th Infantry Division); Major-General Lucian Truscott (3rd Infantry Division) and Patton's deputy, Hugh Gaffey. (NARA)

Patton's Seventh Army, Operation *Husky*: Sicily July 10–August 12, 1943

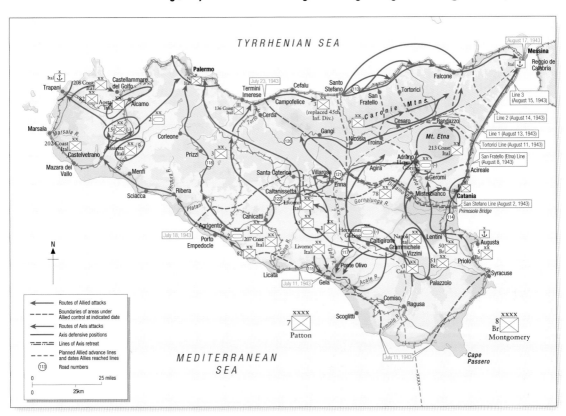

Patton comes ashore on Sicily on July 11, 1943, (D+1) near Gela. To his left is his chief-of-staff Brig. Gen. "Hap" Gay and behind him his new aide-de-camp, Lieutenant-Colonel Charles Codman.

Patton enters Messina in his command car along with Maj. Gen. Lucian Truscott, commander of the 3rd Infantry Division at 1100hrs on August 17, 1943. (NARA)

hospitals, even though the sight of so many badly injured soldiers pained him and undermined his confidence in his own courage. Yet he felt it was a commander's responsibility to do so, and steadfastly continued his hospital tours. On August 3, he visited a 1st Infantry Division hospital and encountered an infantryman with no visible wounds; when asked why he was at the hospital, the young soldier replied, "I guess I can't take it." Patton was infuriated and slapped the soldier with a glove and pushed him out of the tent. He sent a memo to commanders that such men were cowards and that their shirking would lead to court martial for cowardice. The incident was repeated on August 10 against an artilleryman from the 17th Field Artillery who was suffering from combat fatigue and led to such an outburst from Patton that one of the doctors had to intervene to shield the young soldier. Patton showed little understanding of combat fatigue, and his ill-tempered reactions might themselves have been the result of his overwork and stress.

Several correspondents attached to the Seventh Army learned about the incidents, but realizing the sensitivity of the story, reported it to Eisenhower before publishing it. They agreed to sit on the story after Eisenhower promised to deal with the issue. Rebuking Patton in the strongest terms, Eisenhower insisted that he make amends and he apologized to the staffs of the two evacuation hospitals and the soldiers involved. The gentleman's agreement with the press lasted until November 1943 when muckraker Drew Pearson learned of the slapping incidents and broadcast the story on his radio program in the United States. This led to the predictable outcry in the press and Congress, and friends in high places narrowly saved Patton's career. The popular view of Patton after the slapping incidents was of a brutal martinet. Patton believed that his stern discipline was for the soldier's own good. One consequence of the slapping incident was that it made Patton a future target of unscrupulous press attacks.

As Patton's star waned due to his rash behavior, Omar Bradley's star ascended. Bradley had been Patton's deputy in Tunisia and his subordinate on Sicily. The two were polar opposites in temperament and personality, Bradley the dour son of

Missouri sodbusters, a taciturn teetotaler with the cautious persistence of an infantryman. Patton had stepped on Bradley's toes in Sicily as he did nearly all of his subordinate commanders, passing instructions to divisional commanders in Bradley's corps behind his back. Other generals like Lucian Truscott and Terry Allen just took Patton's interference as part of the rough-and-tumble of combat; Bradley harbored a lingering resentment. There were only a handful of plausible candidates to lead the US First Army at Normandy. The Mediterranean campaign had not been kind to many of the "golden boys" on Marshall's list. Fredendall had been sacked after Kasserine, and Mark Clark's performance at Salerno in September 1943, while heroic, left senior commander's suspecting his planning skills. Jacob Devers served as a placeholder in the European command slot, but was not a plausible candidate to lead US troops

Patton felt it his duty to visit wounded troops, and he is seen here on Sicily talking with some men about to be evacuated by ship. During visits later in the campaign, he slapped two enlisted men suffering from shell shock, leading to a public furor that threatened his career. (NARA)

ashore at Normandy due to his lack of combat experience. Other promising candidates such as Robert Eichelberger were already in the Pacific. This left Patton and Bradley, and Patton's reckless behavior pushed him out of contention for the coveted slot. Marshall was adamant on limiting the US contribution in the Mediterranean to a single field army, and with Mark Clark assigned to the Fifth Army slot there were no immediate opportunities for Patton in that theater after Sicily. Patton had redeemed the US Army's reputation in Tunisia and Sicily, but his mercurial temperament had undermined his prospects for higher command. General Marshall may have been right in his aversion to older commanders, even vigorous men like Patton. War is a business best left to the young, and Patton was a decade past his prime.

France: 1944

In spite of the slapping incident, Marshall and Eisenhower knew that they needed a bold cavalryman like Patton for tasks ahead in France. In January 1944, Patton gave up command of Seventh Army and transferred to England, assigned to command Third Army. The plan was to have Bradley command First Army in the initial phase of the Normandy campaign, and then, once the lodgment area was secure, to add Patton's Third Army to expand the American contingent which would then become the 12th Army Group. Once this occurred, Bradley would be elevated to take command of the 12th Army Group, while his deputy Courtney Hodges would take over First Army.

Patton got into trouble again in April 1944 after an innocuous speech in Knutsford to a local community group that was misreported and sensationalized in the American press as a purported insult to the Russian allies. It was nothing of the sort, but many irresponsible reporters looking for a new scandal viewed Patton as fair game. Eisenhower overreacted, but Churchill had long been impressed with Patton and urged calm over such a "tempest in a teapot." The matter quieted down after Patton had been warned yet again "to keep his mouth shut."

Patton built up a loyal staff through his several campaigns. When Geoffrey Keyes was appointed to corps command after Sicily, Hugh Gaffey became his deputy. He is seen here with Patton on August 26, 1944, in France. Patton assigned Gaffey to take over the 4th Armored Division in November 1944 when he was forced to relieve John "Tiger Jack" Wood. (NARA)

The Operation *Overlord* plans for D-Day included a deception operation to convince Berlin that the main Allied landing would occur on the Pas-de-Calais. A fictitious First US Army Group (FUSAG) was created with false radio broadcasts and simulated garrison camps. Patton was nominally in command of FUSAG, playing on the German belief that Patton was their most dangerous adversary.

Patton arrived in France on July 6, 1944, a month to the day after the D-Day landings, his presence and that of his Third Army a top secret. The Normandy campaign had gone slowly for the Allies with Bradley's First Army bottled up in the hedgerow country approaching St. Lô while Montgomery's British and Canadian forces were entangled in fierce tank battles in the open country around Caen. The attrition battle in the hedgerows was gradually shifting in favor of the US Army, and plans were

Bradley and his senior commanders are seen here at a meeting in France in March 1945 to discuss Operation *Lumberjack*. Above him is Patton (Third Army), and to the right Courtney Hodges (First Army), and William Simpson (Ninth Army). (NARA)

Patton's advance: August 1–September 4, 1944

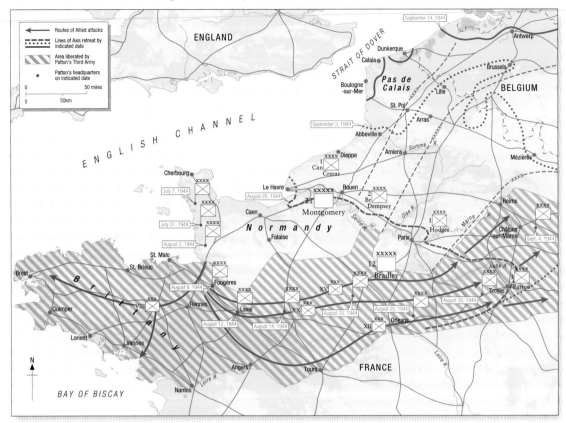

underway for a breakout, codenamed Operation *Cobra*, scheduled to begin on July 24. The aim of the mission was to crack the final crust of German defenses near St. Lô with a carpet-bombing attack, then inject two armored divisions once the penetration had been made. *Cobra* succeeded beyond most expectations, with US units racing deep behind the German lines. The time had come for Patton's Third Army.

The Third Army's mission was part of the original *Overlord* plans to expand the lodgment area westward towards Brittany. The ultimate objective was to secure additional ports in Brittany, notably in the Quiberon Bay area and the port of Brest to assist in the Allied logistics build-up. Patton's drive started on August 1 and was spearheaded by the 4th and 6th Armored Divisions, which made some of the most rapid advances of the war, pushing past weak German defenses at Avranches and breaking into Brittany at a lightning pace. The 4th Armored Division reached Rennes and the 6th Armored Division was soon on the gates of Brest. An essential element in the Third Army's advance was the sterling air support provided by Otto Wayland's XIX Tactical Air Force, one of the classic examples of air-ground cooperation during the war.

In spite of the spectacular advance, Patton was unsettled by the conduct of the campaign and began to question its strategic objectives. His old friend

John S. Wood, commander of the 4th Armored Division, egged him on arguing that the Brittany campaign was an insignificant sideshow. While ports were certainly needed, the Germans had shown at Cherbourg in June that they would demolish the ports before their capture, rendering them useless for months. Furthermore, the Brittany ports were away from the main direction of the Allied advance, adding precious miles to every ounce of supplies that would be delivered through these harbors. If Brittany was an irrelevant objective, Patton at the

The rivalry between Patton and Montgomery has been greatly exaggerated, achieving legendary proportions in the film *Patton*. Bradley held far fiercer views while commanding the US 12th Army Group alongside Montgomery's 21st Army Group in the ETO. (NARA)

same time sensed the real opportunity. The German 7. Armee (AOK 7) was trapped and on the run after *Cobra*, and there was a void in German defenses on the approaches to the Seine River and Paris. A rapid rush to the Seine could help bag German forces in a deep envelopment, while at the same time securing the Normandy lodgment area months earlier than anticipated. Patton argued his case with Bradley and Eisenhower, and won Montgomery's support as well.

The reorientation east was authorized on August 3: Middleton's VIII Corps remained in Brittany to finish the mission against the Breton ports while Wade Haislip's recently arrived XV Corps, spearheaded by the 5th Armored Division, was directed towards Le Mans under Patton's command; Walton Walker's XX Corps and Manton Eddy's XII Corps were to form the southern shoulder of the great mechanized race.

The Wehrmacht was deeply alarmed by the threat posed by this new drive, and attempted to split Hodges' First Army and Patton's Third Army by a Panzer counteroffensive towards Avranches and the sea, codenamed Operation *Lüttich*. The German attack was stopped cold by US infantry at Mortain and proved to be a catastrophic blunder. By shifting their modest Panzer reserves into the American sector, the Germans had fatally weakened the defenses facing Montgomery's 21st Army Group. The Canadian First Army was soon crashing down toward Falaise, and AOK 7 was on the verge of encirclement. While this drama played itself out in the fields of Normandy, Patton's forces were racing eastward against weak German resistance. The tactical situation was a case study for cavalry exploitation, and Patton's bold and risky tactical style was ideally suited to exploit it. Patton urged on his motorized and mechanized spearheads and told them to ignore their flanks. The advance of Hodges' First Army covered the northern flanks, while the Loire River offered a defensive shoulder that could be patrolled by Weyland's XIX Tactical Air Force serving as an airborne cavalry flank guard. The Wehrmacht attempted to shift elements of AOK 1 from the Atlantic coast to block Patton, but Patton's forces were simply much faster. The cities west of Paris fell in rapid succession, including the cathedral cities of Chartres and Orléans, and Paris itself beckoned.

In spite of the enormous success of Patton's August advance, controversies surround the denouement of the campaign. On August 12, Patton suggested swinging his XV Corps on the left flank to help seal off the Falaise Gap near Argentan. Bradley demurred, sending Patton's forces further east to conduct the envelopment along the Seine. The Allied failure to close the Falaise Gap remains one of the war's great controversies, though hardly one for which Patton was responsible. It can certainly be argued that had their places been reversed, then Patton would have favored a more vigorous US Army effort to assist Montgomery in closing the Falaise Gap and enveloping any escaping German forces along the Seine. Instead, Bradley directed Patton's forces south of Paris.

Eisenhower and the Allied commanders were not enthusiastic about liberating Paris so soon. The Allies would then have to take on the responsibilities of feeding its population and this would place a further drain on overstretched Allied logistics. But it was politically impossible to avoid the opportunity. In spite of the role of Patton's Third Army in clearing the way to Paris, the task was handed over to V Corps of First Army since Général Jacques Leclerc's French 2e Division blindée had been earmarked for the liberation of the city for obvious political reasons. Patton's Third Army was directed to the southeast of the capital and toward the traditional gateway into Germany via Lorraine toward Frankfurt.

A very happy Patton meets with Major-General Leroy Irwin, 5th Infantry Division commander, during the Seine river-crossing operation near Fontainebleau south of Paris on August 25, 1944. (NARA)

Patton was the first senior Allied commander over the Seine seen here in his jeep crossing the treadway bridge near Melun on August 26. (NARA)

The Germans later dubbed the final weeks of August and first weeks of September "the void" as their armies in France were in headlong retreat to the German frontier and the Westwall defenses. For Patton, the advance toward Nancy and the German frontier presented a string of familiar sights – his tank battalions had trained and fought in the area during the Great War. But unlike 1918, the advance over the old battlefields was remarkably swift and the casualties light. Though denied the glories of liberating Paris, Patton

Patton is seen with some of his staff here at the Third Army headquarters in Etain France on September 30, 1944. The pugnacious general in the right foreground is Walton Walker, commander of XX Corps, above him and right of Patton is his chief of staff Brig. Gen. Hobart Gay. Left of Patton are his Deputy Chief of Staff for Operations Colonel Paul Harkins, 5th Infantry Division commander Maj. Gen. Leroy Irwin, and Brigadier-General Walter Muller (Third Army G-4). In the foreground is the commander of CCB, 7th Armored Division, Brigadier-General John Thompson. (NARA)

was convinced that destiny awaited him in Lorraine. In August, he had consulted with the distinguished French general Alphonse Juin about the best route into Germany. Juin confirmed what he already believed – the Nancy corridor. Patton remarked to his staff "It is so obvious and such a sure bet, I have no doubt higher headquarters will turn it down." This would indeed be the case as Allied planning continued to focus on the northern routes into Germany through the Netherlands and Belgium.

The September fighting was ultimately a great frustration after the Allies ran out of fuel. Patton's spectacular successes had pushed the Allied front line beyond the Seine and much beyond the expectations of pre-invasion planning. The Allied air campaign against the French rail system had been too successful and it would take months to reconstruct the shattered rail lines and infrastructure. Paris soaked up food and supplies, and Patton's forces were so far from the Normandy ports that it took tremendous amounts of fuel to move supplies to them by truck. In mid-September, Montgomery suggested a bold plan to end the war by using a combined airborne-tank thrust, Operation *Market-Garden*, to seize a Rhine bridgehead at Arnhem in the Netherlands. Taken aback by such an adventurous scheme from the usually conservative British commander, Eisenhower consented. Priority for the limited supplies went to this operation, which ultimately proved too ambitious in the face of hardening German resistance.

Patton was not content to stop and connived to keep his forces moving toward Germany. Captured stocks of German fuel were not reported to higher headquarters, and Patton's logistics chief, Walter Muller, managed to scrounge supplies using unorthodox methods. Muller's "pirates" were reputed to change uniforms and wander into the neighboring First Army sector to divert precious fuel supplies to Third Army. Patton complained that they were stalled because "some son-of-a-bitch who never heard a shot fired in anger or missed a meal believes in higher priorities for pianos and ping-pong sets than for ammunition and gas!"

The Germans were deeply worried by Patton's advance, far more so than the Arnhem operation, which could be contained in the urbanized congestion and flooded farmlands of the Netherlands. The threat posed by Patton's advance southeastward toward Dijon was amplified by Operation *Dragoon*, the US Army and French Army landings on the French Mediterranean coast on August 15. Jacob Devers' 6th Army Group made spectacular headway against the thin German defenses, pushing up the Rhône Valley beyond Lyon and liberating most of southern and central France in a lighting campaign. This left two German armies, AOK 1 and 15 of Heeresgruppe G, in headlong retreat. Patton's advance toward Dijon threatened to cut off the retreating German armies in yet another great encirclement and from the German perspective was a deliberate pincer movement to trap the remainder of the Wehrmacht in France. In fact, there was no such scheme by senior Allied leaders, and the threat was the unintended consequence of Patton's aggressive actions toward Lorraine and the unexpected speed of Devers' 6th Army Group up the Rhône Valley. Hitler ordered another Panzer counteroffensive in hopes of cutting off Patton's thinly spread forces.

However, the momentum of the advances by Patton's Third Army from the north, and Devers' 6th Army Group from the south disrupted Hitler's plans. The great offensive petered out in a series of disjointed Panzer counterattacks, culminating in an inconclusive tank melee around Arracourt in the final weeks of September. Ultimately, the German armies retreating out of southern France lost half their forces, more than 150,000 troops. But the fuel crisis of September 1944 prevented the converging US forces from finishing off Heeresgruppe G.

Patton would later argue that given enough fuel and ammunition, his Third Army could have pushed into Germany and brought the war to a speedier conclusion. While it is certainly true that the German frontier was weakly protected in September 1944, the prospects once Patton reached the Rhine were less assured. In spite of the apparent collapse of the Wehrmacht in September 1944, a substantial rejuvenation was already underway. One of the unpredictable consequences of the fuel problem on the German side was that it made much of the Luftwaffe and Kriegsmarine idle. Large numbers of well-disciplined sailors and aircraft ground crews were suddenly available for conversion into desperately needed infantry. Aside from the sudden swelling of the infantry ranks, the Wehrmacht's arrival back on to German soil led to a fundamental shift in morale. It was one thing to retreat from Belgium and the Netherlands, another thing to give up home and family on native German soil. The fighting spirit returned to the Wehrmacht with a vengeance, and the autumn 1944 campaign would be every bit as bitterly fought as the Normandy battles of the summer.

If August and September 1944 were among the high points of George Patton's military career, October and November were certainly among the grimmest. The autumn of 1944 was one of the rainiest on record, the Moselle reached the flood stage and the fields of Lorraine and the Saar soon turned into a sea of mud. In frustration, Patton later wrote: "I hope that in the final settlement of the war, the Germans retain Lorraine. I can imagine

Patton's preferred mount while commanding the Third Army was a "peep," the Armored Force nickname for a ¼-ton truck instead of the more common "jeep." Patton also had an M20 armored utility vehicle at his disposal and he used it on occasion such as during a tour of the Saar front on November 27, 1944, while escorting the US ambassador to the Soviet Union, Averill Harriman. (NARA)

no greater burden than to be the owner of this nasty country where it rains every day and where the whole wealth of the people consists in assorted manure piles."

Lorraine may have been the traditional invasion path into Germany, but, given Europe's violent history, the province had been heavily fortified over the centuries. The most formidable roadblock was the fortified city of Metz, built and rebuilt by both the French and the Germans as the province frequently changed hands. With more fuel and better weather, Patton might have maneuvered around the fortified zone. Patton's skills as a bold cavalry commander did him little good when faced with the demands of a siege and attritional warfare. Metz did not finally fall until November 22, and the outlying forts held out until December 13 when their defenders faced starvation. Ever the military history buff, Patton reminded his staff, "it was the first time in over four hundred years that the Fortress city had been taken by assault."

There was no more bitter reminder of the frustrations of the autumn fighting than the fate of one of Patton's premier tank commanders, John S. Wood. A fellow cavalryman and old friend of Patton, "Tiger Jack" Wood had led the 4th Armored Division during the race past Avranches and in the swirling tank battles of Arracourt, and had been the inspiration for the glorious race to the Seine. Patton had come to depend on the 4th Armored Division as his spearhead, with the hard-charging Wood as its dynamic leader. But Wood had a testy relationship with his younger XII Corps commander, Manton Eddy. As in the case of the Patton-Bradley relationship, the older and more experienced cavalryman did not see eye to eye with the younger and less adventurous infantryman. Wood had hoped for a corps command, but instead ended up in a situation where a younger officer commanded him. The stress and exhaustion of the autumn fighting took its toll on Wood, who had several angry outbursts with Eddy. The difficulties came to a climax in November when Wood blamed Eddy for the death of a popular junior officer in his division. Eddy insisted that Patton deal with the matter, and Patton was forced to relieve his friend in spite of his obvious talents. The role of the 4th Armored Division in Third Army actions was so critical that Patton had his deputy, Hugh Gaffey, take over the command for the time being.

If Patton's problems at Metz undermine his reputation for bold action, the progress of neighboring armies suggests that the problems were broader and deeper than Patton's Third Army alone. Compared to the problems of Hodge's neighboring First Army in the Hürtgen Forest, Patton's problems

Patton is seen here while visiting the 5th Armored Division near Gossicourt, France, in the early autumn of 1944. He had numerous peeps during his career though this is one of his most significant due to its extensive use while he was in command of the Third Army in 1944–45, registration number W-20339141. Patton liked customized vehicles and, aside from the sirens and rank insignia, this particular peep underwent considerable modification while in Patton's service. The officer in the back is his aide-de-camp, Colonel Charles Codman, while the driver is Sergeant John L. Mims who served with him during the entire war. (NARA)

at Metz pale in comparison. Nor was Bradley's overall direction of the autumn campaign one of his better moments. It is often forgotten that the 12th Army Group expected that Operation *Queen* in November 1944 would be another great breakout akin to *Cobra*; it was a gloomy disappointment. Montgomery's 21st Army Group had its share of frustrations in the autumn, especially the bitter fighting to clear the Scheldt.

The Ardennes

By early December, the port of Antwerp had finally been opened and the supply situation was finally improving. Patton had been hoarding bridging and supplies for a winter offensive, codenamed Operation *Tink*, aimed at Frankfurt and the Rhine. Patton's intelligence chief, Oscar Koch, was keeping an eye out on the left flank in Luxembourg and the Ardennes due to suspicious German activity. There was an unusually heavy amount of rail traffic, and, most ominous of all, the Germans had imposed radio silence on their units in the area. On December 9, Koch warned Patton that the Wehrmacht had amassed sufficient forces in the Ardennes to conduct a large spoiling offensive against the left flank of Operation *Tink*. Patton warned both Bradley and Eisenhower of the German build-up, but Bradley's G-2 dismissed the warnings since he argued the Germans were simply building up their forces on the east bank of the Rhine for a predictable counterattack against Allied efforts against the Rhine scheduled over the next few months. Alone amongst the major commands, Patton's staff was the only one which foresaw the upcoming German attack.

The German Ardennes offensive crashed into Hodges First Army on December 1944, overwhelming the green 106th Infantry Division and pushing the battered 28th Infantry Division back to the road-junction at Bastogne. Bradley called Patton and ordered him to send the 10th Armored Division to Bastogne. Patton groused to his staff: "Our offensive will be called off and we'll have to go up there and save their hides." He ordered his staff to plan for three contingency operations against the flank of the German offensive, and on December 19, he appeared at a conference in Verdun to discuss the situation with Eisenhower, Bradley and the other senior commanders. Eisenhower told him that he wanted a flank attack by six divisions and when he asked Patton when he could begin, Patton said December 21 with three divisions. Eisenhower was taken aback by such a bold proposal and responded "Don't be fatuous, George!" What Eisenhower had overlooked was that Patton's G-2 had already warned of the offensive, the

A meeting on November 13, 1944, at the 4th Armored Division headquarters near Château-Salins to discuss the upcoming Saar offensive. From left to right are Bradley, Maj. Gen. John S. Wood (4th Armored Division), Patton, Maj. Gen. Paul Willard (26th Infantry Division) and Maj. Gen. Manton Eddy (XII Corps). Patton was forced to relieve his old friend "Tiger Jack" Wood several days later after his repeated clashes with Eddy over the conduct of the Saar operations. (NARA)

Patton's relief of Bastogne: December 22–26 1944

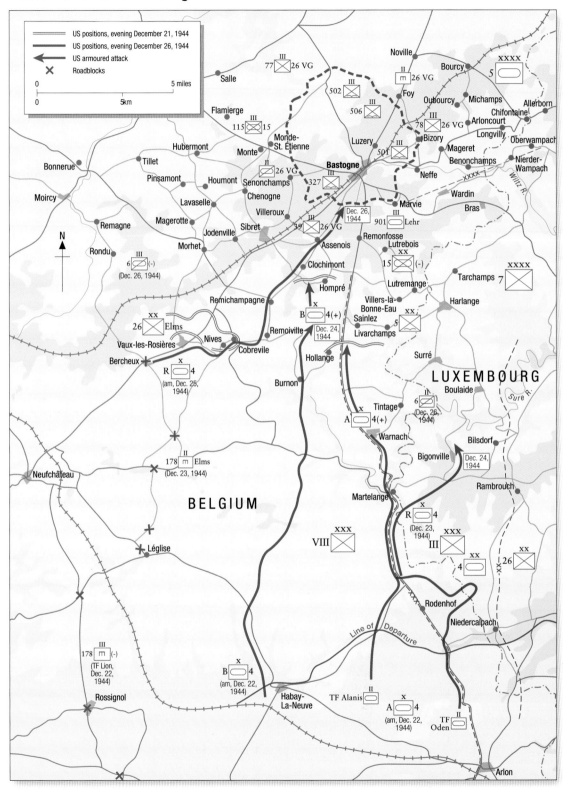

US positions, evening December 21, 1944
US positions, evening December 26, 1944
US armoured attack
Roadblocks

0   5 miles
0   5km

Third Army was already geared up for an offensive on December 18 that would be deferred in favor of the Ardennes mission, and Patton had already assumed that he would be called on to execute precisely such a mission and had told his staff to prepare for it. Patton calmly convinced Ike that he was deadly earnest in his estimate and fully confident that his well-trained units could turn 90 degrees, execute a movement to contact and then stage a meeting engagement against the

Germans somewhere near Bastogne. In his usual colorful fashion, he observed that "The Kraut's stuck his head in a meat-grinder and this time I've got a hold of the handle." Amid the gloom and chill of the Verdun meeting, Patton's optimistic presentation stood out for its brevity, and foresight. Eisenhower quipped to Patton "Every time I get a new star, I get attacked" to which Patton replied "And every time you get attacked, I pull you out," a reference to his role in saving Eisenhower's reputation in Tunisia. Two of Patton's three corps would be committed to the Ardennes, and Patch's Seventh Army to the south would be obliged to extend northward to cover Patton's sector in the Saar. What remained to be seen was whether Patton could indeed engineer such a miracle during the atrocious early winter weather.

Milliken's III Corps moved over a 100 miles (160km), spearheaded by the 4th Armored Division, with the 26th and 80th Infantry Divisions providing the muscle. As Patton promised, the attacks began in the late afternoon of

The calm before the storm. Eisenhower and Bradley meet with VIII Corps commander Troy Middleton in Wilt, Luxembourg, on November 5, 1944. Middleton's corps was assigned to take over the "ghost front" in the Ardennes, also known as the "kindergarten and old-age home" of the First Army as it was composed of newly arrived, green divisions or divisions beaten up in the brutal fighting in the neighboring Hürtgen Forest. Aside from this stint in First Army, Middleton's corps spent most of the war fighting under Patton's command. (NARA)

Congratulations are in order when Ike met with Patton and Bradley in Bastogne on February 5, 1945, following the reduction of the Ardennes bulge. (NARA)

On to Bastogne! Usually a snappy dresser, Patton was a Californian by birth and not fond of the cold weather. He adopted a comfortable but frumpy parka during the frigid January–February 1945 fighting. By this stage, his jeep is sporting new modifications including an armored glass windshield. (NARA)

December 21, with 4th Armored Division reaching to within 13 miles (21km) of Bastogne by the following afternoon. It took four more days of hard fighting before a task force from the 37th Tank Battalion, 4th Armored Division, pushed into Bastogne on December 26, and several more days of intense fighting to create a solid corridor for relief columns to arrive. Combined with a strong push by "Lighting Joe" Collins' VII Corps from the opposite direction, the tide had been turned. The Battle of the Bulge was by no means over, but the Wehrmacht had failed to reach the Meuse River and the momentum was clearly in favor of the US Army. The fighting in the Ardennes would go on for several more weeks in appalling winter weather.

Patton did not win the Battle of the Bulge. First credit must go to the defenders of the First Army – the green but spunky 99th Infantry Division, the infantrymen of the 1st and 2nd Infantry Divisions on Elsenborn Ridge, Bruce Clarke and the 7th Armored Division at St. Vith, the bruised but valiant 28th Infantry Division on the approaches to Bastogne, and, of course, the 101st Airborne Division in Bastogne. But Patton helped inspire and motivate the army in the grim days before Christmas and convince Eisenhower and the other commanders that the German attack was not a calamity, but an opportunity to crush the Wehrmacht. Bradley and Hodges came out of the Ardennes with the reputations badly tarnished for lacking the foresight to anticipate the German attack and for a timid response. Montgomery's contributions were sullied afterwards in a press conference when he took too much credit for too minor a role in the victory. Of the senior commanders, it was Patton's star that shined the clearest and brightest.

Patton's lieutenants

No commander can conduct vast operations without successful subordinates, and Patton had an able selection of corps and divisional commanders. The commanders who he dealt with on a day-to-day basis were his corps commanders. Although Patton would sometimes micromanage and deal

Third Army corps			
Corps	Commander	Attachment to Third Army	Days
XII	Maj. Gen. Manton Eddy	August 1, 1944–May 8, 1945	281
XX	Maj. Gen. Walton Walker	August 1, 1944–May 8, 1945	281
VIII	Maj. Gen. Troy Middleton	August 1–September 5, 1944; December 21, 1944–April 22, 1945	160
III	Maj. Gen. John Milliken	October 10,1944–February 11, 1945; April 18–May 8, 1945	145
XV	Lt. Gen. Wade Haislip	August 1–September 29, 1944	61
V	Maj. Gen. Clarence Huebner	May 6–8, 1945	3

directly with divisional commanders, the standard practice was to conduct the campaign though the corps headquarters. At various times, Patton's Third Army included six corps. Two of these, Eddy's XII Corps and Walker's XX Corps, were with Patton's Third Army during the entire ETO campaign; III and VIII Corps were with Patton for most of the campaign; V and XV Corps were with Third Army for short periods.

Manton Eddy was a considerable contrast to Patton, an infantryman to the bone. He had been commissioned in the Army in 1916 from a small military academy and not West Point, served in infantry units in World War I, and after the war served in a variety of posts including as a tactics instructor at the Command and General Staff School. Compared to other corps commanders, he had not been groomed for higher command and had not attended the Army War College. At the beginning of the war, he was an infantry regiment commander, and at the time of the Tunisia campaign he commanded the 9th Infantry Division. Although the division got off to a rocky start, Eddy soon developed a reputation as a solid commander and came to Patton's attention for his actions both in Tunisia and Sicily. Eddy was transferred from divisional command to head XII Corps on August 19, 1944, when Maj. Gen. Gilbert Cook was relieved for medical reasons. Under Eddy's command, the corps became known as "the Spearhead of Patton's Third Army." During the explosive breakout from Normandy, it was XII Corps that raced to the Seine.

Eddy's XII Corps was one of the two corps that served under Patton for the entire campaign. Although Eddy was an infantryman and not as comfortable as Patton with bold operations, they made a good team. They are seen consulting a map during the Ardennes fighting. (NARA)

Eddy found Patton's daring tactical style a bit uncomfortable. In Normandy, his infantry division had been bitterly battling their way through the hedgerows yards at a time; a mile a day was good progress. When given command of XII Corps, Patton told him his day's objective was 50 miles (80km) behind German lines. He was uncomfortable about advancing so far, so fast with exposed flanks, but Patton told him to ignore the flanks. Unaccustomed to the bold cavalry tactics carried out by armored divisions, Eddy soon came to trust Patton's judgments and to accommodate himself to the new style of war. Nevertheless, his infantryman's perspective would cause tensions with both Patton and his subordinate armored division commanders, most notably with John "Tiger Jack" Wood of the 4th Armored Division. Eddy was well liked by his troops; the legendary journalist Ernie Pyle dubbed him "Old Shoe." The corps played a central role in all of Patton's campaigns, but Eddy returned to the States in April 1945 for medical reasons. After the war, he became commandant of the Command and General Staff School.

Walton Walker was much closer in temperament to Patton, nicknamed "Johnnie" as in Johnnie Walker scotch, or "Bulldog" due to his fierce pug appearance. Patton dubbed him "my fightingest son-of-a-bitch." Walker was a graduate of West Point, class of 1912, and served on the Mexican border in 1916. He was decorated with the Silver Star for gallantry as an infantry officer in France in 1918. During the interwar years he served in a variety of infantry posts, under George Marshall's command at one point. Walker was in the War Plans division when war broke out in Europe in 1939; when the Armored Force was formed in 1940, Walker lobbied Marshall for a transfer to the new branch. He became commander of the 3rd Armored Division in 1942, and later took over IV Armored Corps, which was redesignated as XX Corps in October 1943. Like Patton, he was an energetic, hands-on commander who could usually be found speeding around the front lines by jeep to prod his divisional commanders forward. The XX Corps became nicknamed "the Ghost Corps" after a German prisoner-of-war called Walker's corps by that name in an interrogation because the corps had moved so fast and so often that the Wehrmacht had been unable to keep track of them. During the Ardennes campaign, XX Corps was left behind to cover the Saar and would later spearhead the charge into the Palatinate and across southern Germany. Walker commanded the Eighth Army in Korea, and died in a truck accident in December 1950, five years after Patton's similar death. The new M41 light tank was named the "Walker Bulldog" in his honor.

Walton Walker's XX Corps was the other corps that served under Patton for the entire ETO campaign. Walker is seen here on the right prodding Major-General Lindsay Silvester of the 7th Armored Division outside Chartres on August 19 over the slow pace of the green 7th Armored Division's operation. Like Patton, "Bulldog" Walker was a dynamic and aggressive commander, and during the river crossing at Melun days before, he personally took charge of the 7th Armored Division's river-crossing operations. (NARA)

Troy Middleton was closer to Eddy in temperament than Walker. He served as an infantry colonel in France in 1918, and the later army chief of staff George Marshall wrote in his file "this man was the outstanding infantry regimental commander on the battlefield in France." He served in a variety of senior teaching positions in the army during the interwar years, retiring in 1937 to take up an administrative post at Louisiana State University. He was recalled to duty in 1942 and commanded the 45th Infantry Division on Sicily where he first served under Patton. Eisenhower earmarked him for corps command based on the superb performance of his division there. He later led the division at Salerno, but was nearly forced out of service due to knee problems. His talents were so widely admired that Eisenhower joked that "I'll take him into battle on a litter if we have to" and he was bumped upstairs to command VIII Corps in December 1943. It was under Middleton's command that the 4th and 6th Armored Divisions executed the legendary swing west through Avranches into Britanny in August 1944. After serving with Patton's Third Army through most of the summer campaign, and then the thankless task of clearing the Breton ports, Middleton's corps had the misfortune to be placed in the "quiet sector" of the Ardennes in December 1944 under First Army command where it was hit by the German offensive. The corps returned to Patton's command during the fighting for Bastogne and remained with it through April 1945.

Major-General John Milliken graduated from West Point, class of 1910, and served on staff duties in France in 1918. He served in the cavalry through the interwar years and his leadership of the 6th Cavalry Regiment during the 1940 wargames led to his steady rise to command the 1st Cavalry Brigade and the 2nd Cavalry Division in 1942. The cavalry was a dead-end and after the division was disbanded in North Africa in 1943, Milliken was appointed to lead III Corps. It is interesting to note that Patton had been pushing to get John S. Wood this command instead of Milliken. Alone among Patton's corps commanders, Milliken had never commanded in battle. His corps saw little combat until being assigned to Third Army in October 1944. III Corps' moment of glory came when it was assigned to lead the relief of Bastogne; even if its senior command was still a bit green, it had "Patton's Best," the 4th Armored Division in the lead. The III Corps remained with Patton until March 1945 when Bradley told Patton to shed a corps to First Army; Patton could not bear to lose Middleton and so offered Milliken's III Corps. It was an unhappy marriage with considerable friction between Milliken and Hodges, finally coming to a head after III Corps captured the bridge at Remagen. Hodges relieved Milliken, a decision widely regarded as unwarranted. Ironically, Milliken was later decorated with the Silver Star for his actions at Remagen, and he was given

Major-General John Milliken was not Patton's pick to lead III Corps; he recommended old friend John S. Wood for the slot. Neverthless, Milliken's corps served under Patton from October 1944 through the Ardennes campaign after which it was switched to the First Army. Milliken found it hard to adjust to the different command style in Hodges' First Army and he was relieved in spite of his windfall capture of the Remagen Bridge in March 1945. (NARA)

Although not directly subordinate to Patton, Brigadier-General Otto Weyland's XIX Tactical Air Command was the element of the 9th Air Force attached to Patton's Third Army for close air support. Patton was enormously pleased with Weyland's performance, especially after his harsh criticism of Allied air support in Tunisia and Sicily. (NARA)

command of the 13th Armored Division during the final battles in Germany. Milliken's fate was a clear reminder of Patton's reluctance to relieve commanders. Patton often pointed out that if he had relieved Eddy in Tunisia due to the shaky performance of the 9th Infantry Division, it would have deprived the army of one of its best World War II corps commanders. In spite of his reputation as a fire-breather, Patton was far more patient with his subordinate commanders than Bradley or Hodges. Patton had come close to being relieved on several occasions, and so understood the dilemma better than most.

Although not subordinate to Patton, another general directly associated with Patton's Third Army was Brigadier-General Otto Weyland who commanded XIX Tactical Air Command. This formation was subordinate to the 9th Air Force, but the US Army practice was to assign a tactical air command to each of the armies for close-air support. Patton had been harshly critical of Allied air support in Tunisia and Sicily so his relationship with XIX TAC might have started on a wrong foot. But by Normandy, many of the bugs in the close-air support system had been worked out, and Patton's judgment of the value of air support changed completely. He later dubbed Weyland "the best damned general in the Air Force." Weyland was another Californian, though two decades younger than Patton. He received a commission in 1923 in the Army Air Force (AAF) and originally served in observation units, a forerunner of close-support units. At the start of the war in December 1941, he was a lieutenant-colonel commanding the 16th Pursuit Group in Panama. He became deputy director of air support at HQ AAF in Washington in March 1942, an important step in his eventual combat post. His first combat assignment as a newly minted brigadier-general came in November 1943 when he was assigned to lead the 84th Fighter Wing in Europe. He was transferred to command the new XIX TAC in early 1944 in anticipation of the forthcoming Normandy campaign. XIX TAC flew interdiction missions in support of First Army through July 1944, while at the same time beginning to coordinate with Patton's headquarters for the anticipated activation of Third Army. The performance of XIX TAC in the opening weeks of Operation *Cobra* was so exceptional that Patton placed considerable responsibility on Weyland's unit during the daring advance to the Seine. Instead of dealing with threats to his flanks using conventional forces, Patton turned to Weyland's command to serve as an airborne cavalry screen, keeping an eye on German actions south of the Loire River, and bombing the Loire bridges to keep German forces away from his flanks. The enormous success of XIX TAC in August and September cemented the working relationship between it and the Third Army, and started one of the most successful partnerships of the campaign in the ETO.

The Rhine Rat Race: the Saar-Palatinate triangle, March 12–21, 1945

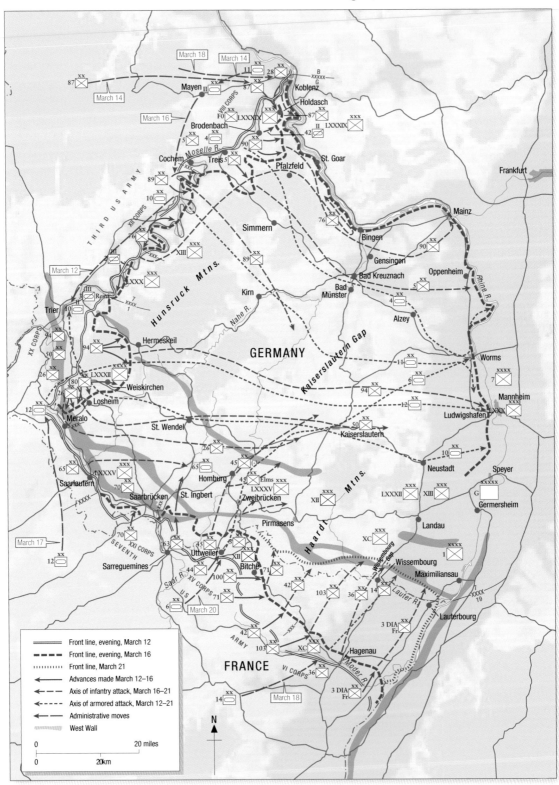

Front line, evening, March 12
Front line, evening, March 16
Front line, March 21
Advances made March 12–16
Axis of infantry attack, March 16–21
Axis of armored attack, March 12–21
Administrative moves
West Wall

0   20 miles
0   20km

N

During the course of the campaign some 42 divisions served at one time or another under Third Army command. This included 25 infantry, 14 armored and 2 airborne divisions. Of these, five are most closely associated with Patton and served nearly the whole campaign under Patton. The 4th Armored Division was frequently dubbed "Patton's best" and served under Third Army every day of the campaign but one; the 6th Armored Division was under Patton for most of the war but the final few weeks. Three infantry divisions served for most of the war under Patton: the 5th, 80th and 90th Divisions. The 90th had the most checkered history, widely viewed as the worst US division in Normandy and nearly broken up for replacements. Yet after a change a leadership, the division turned around and justified their nickname as the "Tough Ombres."

Into the Reich

The late winter campaigns along the German frontier were slow going due to both the weather and the tenacious German defense. Bradley wanted Patton's Third Army on the defensive while the First and Ninth Armies pushed over the Roer in February 1945. Patton's fondness for military history sparked his interest in Trier, a city contested since Roman times. He concocted an "active defense" to take the city using a minimum of forces. He bitterly noted, "I wonder if ever before in the history of war, a winning general had to plead to be allowed to keep on winning." Patton's restless aggressiveness helped Third Army exploit the growing weakness of the Wehrmacht. There were no longer any reserves of manpower to rejuvenate the forces, fuel shortages left the Wehrmacht arthritic and dependent on horses, and its combat power was sapped by shortages of ammunition and broken-down Panzers.

At an impromptu ceremony on March 22, 1945, Patton thanks the engineers who made possible the Third Army's "informal" crossing of the Rhine. (NARA)

One of Patton's most controversial actions in the final campaigns in Germany was the dispatch of a task force from the 4th Armored Division to liberate a prisoner-of-war camp in Hammelburg, 25 miles (40km) behind German lines which contained his son-in-law, Lieutenant-Colonel John Waters. Although initially successful, Task Force Baum eventually succumbed to German counterattacks. (NARA)

This was no more apparent than in the spectacular advances by the Third Army during March's "Rhine Rat Race." On March 12, 1945, the Third Army began an offensive to clear the Palatinate as part of a broader Allied offensive that would culminate in Montgomery's elephantine Operation *Plunder*, the officially sanctioned Rhine crossing, and its associated airborne drop, Operation *Varsity*. Although the German resistance had been stubborn on the first day of the Third Army offensive, within a couple of days both of Patton's corps were advancing over the Moselle against crumbling resistance. After the 90th and 5th Infantry Divisions had advanced 6 miles (10km) beyond the Moselle on 15 March, Patton pushed the 4th Armored Division through them to exploit a yawning gap developing in the German line. Supported by intensive air operations by Weyland's XIX TAC, one of the 4th Armored Division combat commands raced 16 miles (26km) in five hours, and the roving US fighter-bombers kept the Germans from moving reinforcements into the sector. Patton repeated the performance the following day, passing the 10th Armored Division through the 80th and 94th Infantry Divisions to exploit the German predicament. The attack was building up so much momentum, that Eisenhower agreed to give Patton another armored division, the 12th, from the neighboring Seventh

The senior commanders of Patton's Third Army after arriving near Gotha on April 12 along with Ike and Bradley. From left to right are Maj. Gen. Troy Middleton (VIII Corps), Maj. Gen. Walton Walker (XX Corps); Maj. Gen. Van Fleet (III Corps); Patton, Ike and Bradley. (NARA)

Woe to any soldier who violated Patton's rules. The general is seen storming away from an M4A3E8 tank on after having chewed out the crew for the sandbag appliqué armor on their tank, which was against policy in the Third Army. (NARA)

Army to bolster the attack. The 4th Armored Division raced 48 miles (77km) in two days, reaching the banks of the Rhine near Worms, presaging the total collapse of German defense in the Saar-Palatinate triangle in a short one-week campaign.

The "Rat Race" through the Palatinate put Third Army in reach of the Rhine even before Operation *Plunder* ponderously ground forward. On March 7, the 9th Armored Division of Hodges' First Army was the first over the Rhine after securing the Ludendorff Bridge at Remagen. Patton craved a Rhine crossing of his own, all the better if accomplished before Montgomery or Patch's Seventh Army on his right flank. He planned to

Into the Reich: March 1945

Patton holds an impromptu conference with Gen. Dwight Eisenhower, SHAEF commander, and Maj. Gen. Manton Eddy, XII Corps commander. Patton has lent them one of his modified command peeps for a quick tour of the XII Corps sector. Patton always referred to the ¼-ton truck by its preferred Armored Force name, "peep" rather than the more popular name "jeep." This particular peep had been with his headquarters since Normandy and had undergone continual upgrade since the summer of 1944 in the Third Army motor pool. As was typical with most Patton command vehicles, it has a prominent set of sirens on the hood. The command flags are the standard army pattern. The windshield was raised to provide better protection and a transparent plastic visor was added above the top edge for further wind protection. Some improvised doors were also added to the side both for wind protection and to prevent the general or his driver, Sgt. Mims, from getting sprayed with mud. The front fenders have been modified with additional flaps to reduce mud splash. Later in the campaign, armored glass was added to the windshield.

Patton returned briefly to the United States in the summer of 1945 and was given a hero's welcome in several cities including Pasadena, California, as seen here. (NARA)

leap the Rhine on the run without major preparation, and two crossing sites were the most likely. The better of the two was south of Mainz since sites closer to the city involved the crossing of both the Rhine and Main rivers. The Germans recognized this and defenses around Mainz were better prepared. As a result, Patton opted for surprise, and planned the crossing near Oppenheim with a feint at Mainz. On March 22, engineer equipment boats were moved forward to carry the 11th Infantry Regiment of the 5th Infantry Division across that night near Nierstein. German defenses along the Rhine in this sector were meager as AOK 7 was still retreating over the Rhine after its rout in the Saar-Palatinate. The 11th Infantry Regiment set off across the Rhine around 2200hrs, encountering modest German resistance that was quickly overwhelmed. By dawn on 23 March, the 5th Infantry Division had two of its regiments across, followed by a

Following the defeat of Germany, Patton's tasks became more administrative and ceremonial. Here is seen on the reviewing stand with Marshal of the Soviet Union Georgi Zhukov during the September 7, 1945, victory parade in Berlin.

third in the morning and a regiment from the 90th Infantry Division in the evening. The original engineer contingent was swelled with DUKW amphibious truck units, Navy LCVP landing craft and a ferry for tanks. A 40-ton treadway bridge was erected by afternoon. AOK 7 attempted to counterattack but could only scrape up an improvised *Kampfgruppe* from the officer candidate school at Wiesbaden which was brushed off. Patton phoned Bradley: "Brad, we're across!" A muffled exclamation on the other line "Across what,

George?" "The Rhine... and you can tell the world Third Army made it before Monty." To needle Montgomery, Patton announced the success of the crossing the day before Montgomery's planned operation, pointing out that the Third Army could cross the Rhine even without artillery preparation, never mind a full-blown airborne assault. Later in the day, Patton traversed the Rhine bridge, and, in his usual theatrical fashion, urinated into the river. On reaching the east bank, he faked a stumble, ending up with both hands full of dirt. "Thus William the Conqueror!" another bit of theatre recalling William's remark nine centuries before "See! I have taken England with both hands!"

Even in triumph, Patton continued to display a penchant for getting into trouble. In late March, Patton learned that his son-in-law, Lieutenant-Colonel John Waters, who had been captured during the 1st Armored Division's disastrous combat actions at Kasserine Pass, was probably in the Oflag XIIIB prisoner camp in Hammelburg about 40 miles (64km) behind German lines. Feigning ignorance of Waters presence, Patton ordered the 4th Armored Division to send a task force to liberate the camp. Task Force Baum set off on the night of March 26 and did manage to reach the camp and liberate the prisoners. However, the small task force could only carry about 250 of the 5,000 prisoners and three Wehrmacht divisions quickly closed in on the small force and crushed it. The survivors were rounded up and put back in the Hammelburg camp. The raid had been a pointless waste of men and in the event the camp was liberated hardly a week later by the 14th Armored Division from the neighboring Seventh Army. Although roundly criticized for the raid, Patton was spared from any official recriminations due to the attention focused on the death of President Franklin Roosevelt on April 12. The press soon found other subjects when Third Army liberated the gruesome concentration camps at Ohrdruf and Buchenwald.

The advance of the Third Army through southern Germany had been so rapid that after most of the US Army was ordered to a halt on the Elbe River, Eisenhower instructed Patton to continue east. Third Army reached the Czech border on May 4, and Patton asked permission to liberate Prague. Eisenhower consented to an advance as far as Plzen (Pilsen), but Bradley had to restrain him from moving any further east.

Press controversies dogged Patton through the summer and autumn of 1945 and led to his eventual relief as Third Army commander in October 1945 and his transfer to the Fifteenth Army slot. Seen behind him is his replacement, Lt. Gen. Lucian Truscott who he had commanded on Sicily and who went on to corps command at Anzio in 1944. In the far background is his old friend, Lt. Gen. Ernie Harmon. (NARA)

The final parade. Patton's flag-draped casket is taken by half-track from Christ Church, Heidelberg, to a train for internment at a military cemetery with other Third Army soldiers in Luxembourg on December 23, 1945. Leading the honor guard is Master Sergeant William Meeks who was Patton's orderly for eight years. (NARA)

Following the conclusion of the war, Third Army was garrisoned in Bavaria and Patton was assigned the task of military governor. It was a task for which he was ill suited. His trusted staff gradually faded away as they returned to the United States or to other army assignments. Patton's anti-Soviet attitudes, a string of anti-Semitic remarks relating to the refugees in the displaced persons camps and an apparent toleration for Nazis in the local Bavarian Government all brought unfavorable press attention. Patton bluntly stated what the other occupation officials discretely hid, that it was impossible to administer postwar Germany without former Nazi officials since so many government officials had been party members. Patton's misfortune was to state it more bluntly than most, and, worse yet, to members of the press who relished another Patton controversy. In September 1945, Eisenhower relieved Patton of Third Army command, sending him instead to the backwater of Fifteenth Army in Bad Neuheim. On December 9, 1945, Patton took a short trip with a new driver towards Mannheim; his wartime driver had returned to the States. Shortly before noon, his 1939 Cadillac Model 75 had a collision with an army truck at a speed of about 30mph (48kmph). Patton was in the back seat and was thrown forward, causing head injuries and snapping his neck. Patton lingered in hospital for 12 days before finally dying on December 21, 1945. He was buried alongside other Third Army soldiers in the Hamm military cemetery near Luxembourg City in the Ardennes on Christmas Eve, a year after the battle that made him so famous.

Patton's tanks

Patton and Rommel are two World War II commanders who are generally regarded as "tank generals." Yet senior commanders, even those in charge of tank divisions, seldom operated from tanks.

Patton's earliest contact with tanks was in late 1917 when he was assigned to establish the Langres tank school. While Patton undoubtedly drove around in the Renault FT tanks to become acquainted with them, he did not regularly command from a tank. French Renault tank battalions were nominally equipped with a "char signal" radio tank equipped with an early and primitive E10 radio. However, these were in short supply and the radio was unreliable. As a result, Patton did not regularly operate with this type of vehicle when in combat. As a brigade commander, Patton's usual links to his subordinate tank battalions were by field telephone when operating under relatively static conditions, or the traditional method of runners

Patton's Third Army: September 1944–May 1945

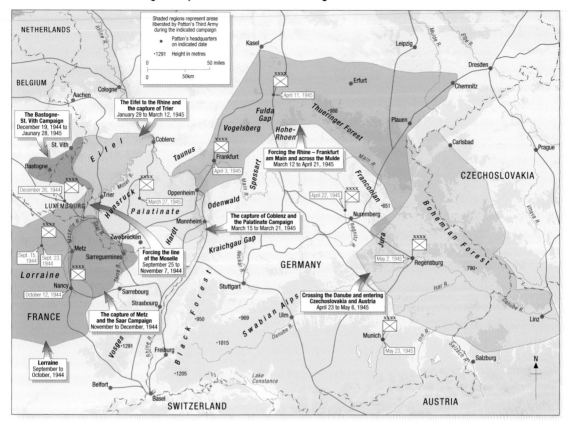

during mobile operations. Patton's commanding officer, Brigadier-General Samuel Rockenbach, expected Patton to command his tanks in the usual fashion, remaining behind at the headquarters and directing the tanks by using messengers. Patton could not refrain from being in the thick of the fight, so he ignored Rockenbach's instructions and commanded from the front. The early tanks were quite slow, hardly the speed of a walking soldier in any type of rough terrain. So Patton could walk behind the tanks during their advance. Patton's personal solution to the communication problem was to carry a walking stick and to run over to a tank and smack the back turret hatch with the cane to get the commander's attention. Once the hatch opened, Patton would then shout any instructions to the tank commander. Like the tanks themselves, this method was primitive and dangerous. Patton's bold and risky command style when leading these tanks was the reason he was wounded.

Patton had little contact with tanks in the interwar years, until he was assigned to command the 2nd Armored Brigade of the 2nd Armored Division in July 1940. This was one of the rare occasions when he actually operated from a tank. He was assigned an M1A1 Light Tank, which previously had the cavalry designation of M2 Combat Car until the consolidation of the infantry tanks and cavalry combat cars under the unified Armored Force in the summer

Left: Patton used an M1A1 light tank while in command of the 2nd Armored Brigade, and later the 2nd Armored Division at Ft. Knox. He is seen here during the wargames in Georgia in September 1941. Riding with him to his right is Brigadier-General Willis Crittenberger, who took over command of the 2nd Armored Brigade when Patton moved to divisional command. (NARA)

Right: Patton as tanker. This portrait was taken of Patton in 1940 as a brigadier-general in command of the 2nd Armored Brigade at Ft. Knox. He is wearing ordinary HBT tanker's coveralls with the prewar style of the tanker's helmet. (NARA)

of 1940. Patton obviously enjoyed riding around in this vehicle at Ft. Knox and there are ample photos showing him in or around this tank. When he took over divisional command, he kept this tank as his personal mount. However, when Patton was actually out in the field exercising command, he seldom used this light tank. Although it did have a radio, the early AM radios fitted in these tanks were not very reliable and could not be used when the tank was in motion. A more practical command vehicle was an M3A1 scout car, essentially an open-topped armored truck. The advantage of this vehicle was that it could contain several radios to cover all the communication bands within the division, since subordinate units operated on a variety of frequency bands. The same was the case with his ostensible German counterpart, Erwin Rommel. Rommel did not operate from a tank during his famous leadership of the 7. Panzer-Division in France in 1940. He operated from an SdKfz 251 command half-track equipped with a variety of radios and encryption devices. Patton had his scout car modified by the addition of sirens, a trademark that would be seen on many of his later command vehicles. Patton wanted his troops to know that he was present, and he enjoyed racing around Ft. Knox with the siren wailing. This was part of the reason his troops dubbed him the "Green Hornet."

Patton left his obsolete M1A1 Light Tank behind at Ft. Knox when he departed for the Desert Training Center in Ft. Irwin, California, in 1941. At the DTC, Patton sometimes operated from a newer M3 light tank, better known by its British nickname of "Stuart" after the Confederate Civil War cavalry commander. Patton kept a light tank at his disposal for show more than for practical reasons. A divisional commander had no particular need for a tank, and the small size of the US Army light tanks limited the

Patton's staff modified an M3A1 scout car for his use while commander of I Armored Corps in North Africa. He used it in Tunisia and Sicily. (NARA)

number and size of radios that could be carried. His DTC light tank was part of Patton's "war face," his deliberate effort to accent his military leadership with all manner of bellicose uniforms, weapons and equipment. When not posing for the camera, Patton usually operated from a variety of other command vehicles including "peeps," the preferred cavalry name for ¼-ton trucks and better known elsewhere in the army as jeeps. He also operated from command cars, usually the standard ¾-ton type, from staff cars and from the M3A1 scout car.

Much the same was true when Patton went overseas in command of I Armored Corps in Morocco in November 1942. At this point, Patton gave up all pretense of operating from a tank. His aides modified a M3A1 scout car for his use when he visited the front lines. This had additional armored shields on the front and rear, and the scout car was ostentatiously festooned with no fewer than three .50-cal. heavy machine guns instead of the usual one. As a concession to the more practical communication needs of a senior commander, this vehicle also had an ample array of command radios in a special console added in the center of the vehicle for Patton.

A far more practical vehicle for a senior commander was the Dodge ¾-ton reconnaissance car, which, contrary to its designation, was used primarily as a command car. (NARA)

Patton regularly used a Dodge ¾-ton reconnaissance car and his vehicle was modified in Britain in May 1944 for his subsequent use in France. Besides the pedestal-mounted .50-cal. heavy machine gun evident on this side, the command car also had an armored plate in front of the radiator and a pair of siren horns on the right fender. (NARA)

This scout car stayed with him when he went on to command II Corps in Tunisia after the Kasserine debacle, and again to Sicily when he commanded the Seventh Army.

In North Africa, Patton regaled the press with his usual tall tales of military derring-do, a particular favorite being a challenge to Rommel. According to the press accounts, Patton suggested that he and Rommel draw up their armies like a feudal tournament, and then the two champions would meet on the field of battle, each like armored knights in their own tanks, to decide the fate of the campaign. This was of course fanciful nonsense, but it delighted the press and the general public. In April 1943, Patton's portrait was on the cover of *Time* magazine as the hero of the hour, the taunt of the medieval tank joust was featured again in the cover story. Neither Patton nor Rommel had ever fought from a tank in combat nor would they ever do so. After the war, one of Patton's best tank commanders remarked "Patton knew as little about tanks as anyone I knew." The same was true about Rommel. Neither commander was especially interested in the technicalities of tank design. They were primarily concerned about their tactical potential on the battlefield.

As in Patton's case, Rommel did not operate from a tank during the North Africa campaign. He used a radio-equipped SdKfz 250 light half-track nicknamed Greif (Griffon). However, during the course of the fighting the Afrika Korps captured three British AEC Dorchester armored command vehicles. These resembled a large armored bus and were a very practical staff vehicle for senior commanders due to their large size, which permitted an ample array of radios, but also convenient areas for the stowage and display of battle-maps. Rommel subsequently used these "Mammuts," renamed Max and Moritz, as mobile command posts.

Although Patton had his M3A1 scout car with him in Sicily, he began to turn increasingly to the use of a more practical ¾-ton reconnaissance car, a version of the widely used Dodge ¾-ton truck. Most photos of Patton

Patton periodically used light observation aircraft for travel in France to avoid the frequent traffic jams during the race to the Seine. Here is seen in August 1944, using a Stinson L-5 Sentinel of the 14th Liaison Squadron to visit forward troops. This squadron was attached to Patton's Third Army headquarters and operated 32 of these light aircraft. (NARA)

traveling in Sicily show him in this vehicle. One of the reasons for the switch to more conventional transport was his age. By 1943, Patton was 57 years old and he had suffered a number of riding injuries in the 1930s. Tanks and scout cars were very difficult to enter and exit; a command car was a far more comfortable vehicle to ride in, and faster as well.

Patton did not regularly operate from an armored vehicle after Sicily. His two preferred mounts in tactical settings were either a ¼-ton peep (jeep) or a ¾-ton Dodge command car. His staff modified these to suit his whims. Both received sirens, a Patton trademark since his "Green Hornet" days at Ft. Knox in 1941. To give the staff car a more bellicose appearance, a pedestal-mounted .50-cal. heavy machine gun was added. His staff gradually modified these vehicles for Patton's safety and comfort, including various mudguards and armored glass for the windshield. In rear area settings, Patton generally traveled in a large staff car, a 1939 Cadillac Model 75 being his preferred steed and it is preserved to this day at the Patton Museum at Fort Knox.

Appropriately enough, Patton became the namesake of the US Army's Cold War armored workhorses, the M47 and M48 medium tanks. In keeping with the British tradition of naming new US tanks after famous US generals, the US Army adopted the practice in the late 1940s and Patton was the second general so-honored, the earlier M26 having been named after Patton's mentor, General John "Black Jack" Pershing.

OPPOSING COMMANDERS

Popular legend sees Rommel as Patton's arch-nemesis. In fact, neither general faced each other on the field of battle. The legend arose from the fact that Rommel was one of the few German commanders who were well known

The diminutive and dynamic Prussian Panzer general Hasso von Manteuffel, seen here to the left, was probably the closest analog to Patton in the Wehrmacht fighting in France and Germany in 1944–45. He fought against Patton in Lorraine and the Saar in the autumn of 1944 in command of the 5. Panzerarmee, but his claim to fame came for his brilliant leadership during the Ardennes offensive where his units cracked the US lines near Bastogne. In the center is Generalleutnant Horst Stumpf, inspector of the Panzer force on the Western Front. To the right is Generalfeldmarschall Walter Model, commander of Heeresgruppe B, who was Bradley's counterpart on the German side during the Ardennes campaign. (US Army MHI)

during World War II and today to the English-speaking audience. It is hard to get excited about a contest between Patton and Brandenburger, when most of the audience has no idea who Brandenburger was during the war. Nor is the Rommel-Patton comparison entirely appropriate even had they faced each other in Tunisia or France, as Rommel was generally one step ahead of Patton in rank. In Tunisia, Rommel was a field army commander, Patton a mere corps commander; when Patton was a field army commander in France, Rommel was already an army group commander.

Modern warfare seldom pits a corps or field army neatly against another comparable formation and its commander. For example, in Tunisia Patton's II Corps fought against Arnim's 5. Panzerarmee, which included elements of an Italian and a German corps; likewise Patton's opponents in Sicily were an assortment of German and Italian units. Patton's Third Army faced an incredibly motley selection of units in August 1944 when it burst on the scene in the wake of Operation *Cobra*. The Third Army's opponent in Brittany was XXV Armeekorps (AK) commanded by General der Artillerie Wilhelm Fahrmbacher. He had commanded the 5. Infanterie-Division in Poland in 1939 and in France in 1940, and was appointed to command VII AK on occupation duty in France in 1940. He led this corps during Operation *Barbarossa* in Russia in the summer and autumn of 1941, but was assigned to XXV AK on occupation duty in France in May 1942. On August 1, 1944, he was appointed commander of all German troops in Brittany but it was a vain attempt to unify command over a disparate assortment of naval troops in the Breton ports and the handful of army units that had not already been sent into the maelstrom of Normandy. Patton's forces quickly overran most of Brittany, but three ports held out: Brest, Lorient and St. Nazaire. After a costly campaign to overwhelm the port of Brest in September 1944, the US Army decided to simply let the two remaining "fortress ports" wither on the vine, and Fahrmbacher did not surrender Festung Lorient until after Berlin capitulated in May 1945.

When Patton's Third Army swung east in mid-August towards Paris and the Seine, it faced little organized opposition. With AOK 7 and the 5. Panzerarmee trapped near Falaise, the headquarters of AOK 1 in Bordeaux was assigned the impossible task of attempting to control operations in the Loire Valley. As an expedient, the AOK 1 headquarters' Ia (operations section) under Oberstleutnant Emmerich was sent to form a regional headquarters at Fontainebleau, later dubbed "General z.b.V. AOK 1" (z.b.V.= *zur besonderen Verwendung:* for special purpose) but its motley units were steamrollered by the onrush of Patton's Third Army.

Patton's old adversary, the 5. Panzerarmee, was resurrected in France in 1943 after it had been destroyed in Tunisia. It was crushed again in Normandy in the Falaise Gap in August 1944, and resurrected yet again in September to take part in the swirling Panzer counterattack against Patton in Lorraine in September 1944. It was led by Hasso von Manteuffel, one of the most successful German commanders on the Western Front and the only German commander who faced Patton in 1944–45 of comparable stature. Manteuffel served in World War I and switched to the new Panzer branch in 1934, commanding an infantry battalion in Rommel's 7. Panzer-Division in France in 1940. He was awarded the Ritterkreuz for his action in seizing a bridgehead during the Moscow fighting in November 1941. He later fought in the North Africa campaign and Arnim described him as one of his best divisional commanders in Tunisia. Hitler personally assigned him command of the 7. Panzer-Division in June 1943, and, later in the year, transferred him to lead the elite Panzergrenadier-Division 'Großdeutschland' after being decorated with the Oakleaves for the Ritterkreuz. Manteuffel's growing battlefield reputation and personal contacts with Hitler led to his steady advancement. On September 1, 1944, he was called to the Führer's headquarters and ordered to take command of the 5. Panzerarmee, thus leapfrogging from divisional to army commander in a single step, and bypassing the usual stage as a Panzer corps commander. In spite of his sudden advancement in rank, Manteuffel was faced with insuperable problems in executing Hitler's ambitious plans to cut off Patton's Third Army. The forces that were allotted to the offensive did not arrive in time or had already been frittered away in attempts to hold the line in Lorraine before the start of the attack. As a result, Manteuffel's attacks were disjointed and ultimately ineffective.

By the end of September, Patton had run out of fuel and Manteuffel had run out of troops and Panzers. A bloody stalemate ensued in Lorraine with two of Patton's corps facing the remnants of 5. Panzerarmee near Saarebourg, and

Patton's adversary in the Ardennes was Erich Brandenberger, commander of the German AOK 7. (MHI)

one corps facing AOK 1 around Metz. AOK 1 had been reconstituted after its retreat from the Atlantic coast at Bordeaux and put under the command of General der Panzertruppe Otto von Knobelsdorff on September 5, 1944. Knobelsdorff had commanded 19. Infanterie-Division in France in 1940 and led 19. Panzer-Division in the invasion of Russia in 1941, receiving the Ritterkreuz in September 1941. He distinguished himself as a Panzer corps commander in the attempts to relieve Stalingrad and was personally appointed by Hitler due to his bravery and unflinching optimism. Senior German commanders felt that his tactical skills were unimpressive, and he was in poor physical shape after grueling Eastern Front duty when assigned to the Saar front. Knobelsdorff may not have been one of the Wehrmacht's best field army commanders, but in view of the dismal weather and the heavy fortifications around Metz, he was able to hold off Walker's XX Corps for the better part of two months. Knobelsdorff lasted until the end of November 1944 when he was relieved by Hans von Obstfelder, another Eastern Front veteran but a decade younger. Obstfelder formerly commanded XXIX AK in Russia through the middle of 1943 before being transferred to France to lead LXXXVIII AK. This corps fought in Normandy in the Caen sector and was decimated in the Falaise Gap.

The 5. Panzerarmee disappeared from in front of Patton's Third Army in a reshuffle of the Wehrmacht defenses in the Saar. Manteuffel and the 5. Panzerarmee had been assigned one of the lead roles in the upcoming Ardennes offensive, attacking Middleton's VIII Corps. It was Manteuffel's astute leadership that resulted in the main breakthrough in the Battle of the Bulge near Bastogne; the other main thrust by Dietrich's 6. Panzerarmee got hung up by the stubborn American defense on Elsenborn Ridge and St. Vith.

When Patton launched the Third Army counterattack into the Ardennes, the main opponent was not the 5. Panzerarmee, but Erich Brandenberger's AOK 7, the weakest of the three German armies taking part in the attack. Brandenberger had none of Manteuffel's flashy brilliance, and the overall commander of the Ardennes offensive, Generalfeldmarschall Walter Model, deprecated him as "a typical product of the general staff system." In spite of Model's snide assessment, Brandenberger had served as commander of a Panzer division and later a corps on the Eastern Front and was a solid performer throughout the autumn-winter 1944–45 campaign.

Patton's Third Army remained ensnared with AOK 7 through the end of the war in May 1945, but there was a game of musical chairs in this German field army as Patton's units ground through the Wehrmacht defenses. Brandenberger was replaced by General der Infanterie Hans Felber on February 22, who lasted only a month due to the disastrous rout of AOK 7 in the Palatinate. He was replaced by Gen. Hans von Obstfelder who had taken over Felber's AOK 19 command a month earlier; Brandenberger switched to AOK 19.

Very little has been made of any rivalry between Patton and these German commanders, as they are largely faceless and unknown outside Germany. Comparisons between Patton and his German adversaries confront the usual problems of "apples versus oranges." On the one hand, the German commanders had far more combat experience than Patton. Nearly all of these commanders were World War I veterans, and had served in combat for nearly four years in the Polish, French and Russian campaigns. There may be an issue of when "battle-hardened" becomes "battle-weary," but clearly these were highly experienced and skilled commanders. Patton had seen barely two months of combat when the Third Army entered the field in France in August 1944. The German officers suffered under the daunting problems confronting the Wehrmacht in late 1944–45 when facing the US Army. There was a perpetual shortage of fresh troops, impossible shortages of fuel and artillery ammunition, and a decimated Panzer force. The Allies enjoyed air superiority for most of the campaigns, while Luftwaffe air support was a rarity. Patton enjoyed the advantage of leading a far better equipped and more modern force, and never faced the desperate circumstances confronting his Wehrmacht opponents. On the other hand, the German commanders had their own advantages, though seldom enough to tip the balance in their favor. Patton's Third Army was almost invariably on the offensive, and modern warfare usually requires a preponderance of force to overcome a good defense; there can be no doubt that the Wehrmacht was a formidable defensive force, even its emaciated state in 1944–45. In the autumn of 1944, the German commanders enjoyed the defensive advantages of miserable weather, which often grounded US air support and limited the mobility of US forces due to mud.

It is easier to compare "like to like" and in this respect, Patton had a shining record. Third Army captured more ground and more prisoners than any other field army in the ETO campaign, and the Wehrmacht singled out Patton as their greatest threat.

Patton's command	Operation	Date	Opposing force	Commander
Western Task Force	Operation *Torch*	November 1942	French Division de Casablanca	M. E. Béthouart
II Corps	Operation *Wop*	March 1943	Elements of 5. Panzerarmee	Hans-Jürgen von Arnim
Seventh Army	Operation *Husky*	July 1943	Italian Sixth Army	Alfredo Guzzoni
Third Army	Operation *Cobra*	August 1944	Scattered units	
Third Army	Lorraine	September 1944	5 Panzerarmee	Hasso von Manteuffel
Third Army	Metz and Saar	October–November 1944	AOK 1, 5. Panzerarmee	Otto von Knobelsdorff
Third Army	Ardennes	December 1944–January 1945	AOK 7	Erich Brandenberger
Third Army	Palatinate	February–March 1945	AOK 7	Hans Felber
Third Army	Frankfurt and Rhine	March 1945	AOK 7	Hans von Obstfelder
Third Army	Bavaria-Czechoslovakia	April–May 1945	AOK 7	Hans von Obstfelder

Patton in his milieu, observing the battle for El Guettar in Tunisia in March 1943 from a nearby hillside. (NARA)

INSIDE THE MIND

Patton was a military intellectual, an avid student of military history and a frequent contributor to military journals on a wide range of subjects. His professional military education was not much different than most other senior US Army commanders during the war, but Patton extended his studies far beyond the army educational system with extensive reading both of the military classics and contemporary writings on defense affairs. If the interwar US Army tended to focus on the lessons of recent wars, Patton viewed war as a timeless human endeavor; the wars of antiquity held clues as valuable to unlocking its secrets as recent conflicts. Prior to the campaign in France, he studied the Norman Conquest, assuming that the roads used in the times of William the Conqueror remained the best avenues nearly a millennia later.

Patton fell outside of the mainstream of US Army military thinking in many respects. The interwar US Army saw modern warfare shaped by a military revolution of technology and industrial power. Mass conscript armies would fight modern war, and the face of modern war would be shaped by modern technology. The enormous impact of firepower technology was painfully evident in World War I, distorting the balance between offense and defense. This viewpoint led to the emergence of a new style of military leadership, dubbed the "managerial" style in recent years. The modern commander was no longer seen as a heroic figure leading the army forward into battle with his charismatic presence. Instead, the commander's place was in the rear, managing his staff, planning his operations with precision, thinking deeply about future operations, monitoring the lifeblood of his army's logistics. While bravery was not discounted, calm intellectual prowess was the cardinal virtue. Eisenhower and Bradley clearly fit within this mold of the "organization man," and it helps to explain their success in attaining senior leadership.

Patton's perspective on command was very different – a traditional focus on romantic and heroic leadership. He wrote "There is a regrettable and widespread belief among civilians and in the Army that we will win this war through materiel. In my opinion, we will only win this war through blood, sacrifice and high courage." He placed great importance on personal courage, and on numerous occasions deliberately placed himself in harm's way both to test his own mettle as well as to display it to both his men and his superiors. Patton believed in leadership by example, of leading from the front, of exerting a strong personal imprint on his operations. He was wounded in 1918 while disobeying his commander's instructions to remain in the rear. In his view, a commander needed a "warrior soul," a strong blend of courage, energy, boldness, and self-confidence. Beyond the personal virtues that this entailed, Patton believed it necessary that a leader convey this martial spirit to his troops. In his early days as a junior officer, he began creating a military persona, what he called his "war face." Patton viewed the talents of an actor as an essential element in leadership. He patterned his scowl after the legendary cold face of Black Jack Pershing. In view of his genteel upbringing, his fluorescent profanity was a complete affectation to distract from a high-pitched voice that he viewed as unmanly. He varied his persona to his audience: in the presence of fellow officers he was professional; in front of his men he was gruff, inspirational and vulgar; in front of women he was a model of courtesy and suave civility. It is often difficult to separate Patton the actor from the real Patton. One minute he could be a fire-breathing autocrat lashing out at his subordinates, the next minute a maudlin sentimentalist crying at the sight of wounded soldiers in a field hospital. Acting or a lack of self-control? Omar Bradley characterized Patton as a Jekyll and Hyde.

The US military education system of the interwar years was preparing its senior commanders to shape American strategy and defense policy. This did not interest Patton who continued to argue that that success at the cutting edge of battle was more important than planning. His focus remained concentrated on the operational art of war and on the evolution of military tactics. While this made Patton a first-rate divisional and corps commander, his perspective also helps explain why he did not advance beyond field army command during the war. While his lack of self-control was the immediate cause of his problems in 1943, it is by no means clear that Eisenhower or Marshall viewed Patton as the ideal candidate for the army group commands eventually given to Bradley and Devers. Eisenhower was always skeptical of Patton's abilities to plan beyond the tactical level, and after the war attributed

Like many traditional commanders of the romantic mold, Patton was a consummate actor. He practiced his "war face" in front of the mirror, and here displays his trademark scowl while posing for army photographers after the El Guettar battle in Tunisia in 1943. Patton once told his aide: "I wish to hell I had a fighting face; you are either born with one or not. Having practiced hours in front of the mirror, I can work up a fairly ferocious expression, but I have not got, and never will have, a natural-born fighting face." (NARA)

some of Patton's successes to his execution of Bradley's plans, not solely to his own actions. The skills of a fine tactical commander were not necessarily those of a strategic commander.

Patton's tactical style favored shock and bold action over attrition and firepower. An enemy off balance was far more vulnerable than an enemy saturated with indiscriminate artillery fire. It was a cavalryman's perspective in an army led more often than not by infantry officers.

Although Patton is closely associated with modern tank warfare, he was never especially interested in modern military technology. "Patton knew as little about tanks as anyone I knew," wrote General Bruce Clarke who served under Patton leading a combat command of the 4th Armored Division in the summer and autumn of 1944. Clarke was referring to his technical understanding, not Patton's tactical skills with tanks. Patton's success with tank warfare was due to his appreciation of tanks as a tool that had to serve the traditional arts of war, not some sort of miracle weapon. Patton's facility with tanks was most evident when employing armored divisions as a mobile exploitation force – essentially a mechanized equivalent of traditional horse cavalry. Patton was not a maverick and had little to do with the mechanization of the army in the interwar years. Both he and Eisenhower had been warned off from promoting a separate tank branch in 1920, and Patton realized that acting as a prophet of mechanization would not help his chances of career advancement in the cavalry. Even in the late 1930s, he was still trying to redesign the perfect cavalry saber.

Patton did not discount technology but he did not believe in its primacy in warfare. "Moral force is the soul of battle," not military hardware. In his view, the traditional demands of war took precedence: training, morale, discipline. Nor was he a big fan of the citizen-soldier, preferring a professional force if at all possible. It was not possible and so Patton had to make do with conscripts. Many senior American military leaders had a sentimental belief in the innate military talents of the American citizen-solider as inherently self-reliant and aggressive. Patton was skeptical of these civic pieties and believed

Patton was aggressive and offensively minded. As a result, he was especially fond of tactical bridging since no advance was possible in Europe without a crack engineer force able to quickly bridge the numerous rivers that would otherwise hold up an advance. He is seen here on February 20, 1945, posing with troops of the 1303rd Engineer Battalion who had recently completed this bridge over the Sauer River. (NARA)

that traditional military training and discipline was absolutely vital to break down civilian ways of thinking and to prepare men for the savagery of modern war. Patton's rationale was incisive: "If you can't get them to salute when they should salute, and wear the clothes you tell them to wear, how are you going to get them to die for their country?" American popular culture after World War I was strongly anti-militaristic, so Patton's attitude did not go over well with many conscripts, and was a frequent bone of contention with the press.

Patton was a bundle of paradoxes. A devout Episcopalian, yet a casual believer in reincarnation. A solicitous commander who often visited field hospitals, yet capable of striking and bullying a shell-shocked soldier. An able diplomat in his delicate dealings with the French in Tunisia, but politically tactless in occupied Germany. Patton's main intellectual weakness was that he was overwhelmingly self-centered and too often viewed the world as an extension of himself. He reveled in "bad boy" behavior, having managed since childhood to avoid the consequences. Patton's paradoxes make him a fascinating character, and no doubt have accounted for his enduring place in American popular culture.

Shortly after the war his wartime aide, Charles Codman, described Patton's paradoxes: "The tough vocabulary, the emphasis on frightfulness, the simulated rages, so many symptoms of the conflict between his inner nature and the demands of his chosen medium.... There are signs already the old gory legend of the profane, hard-drinking, hard-living primitive is beginning to wear thin, and since upon inspection even its superficial aspects fail to pass muster, future biographers and historians should have little difficulty piercing its speciousness."

A rare photo of Patton in a jovial mood during a postwar visit with his old friend Jimmy Doolittle, the noted aviator and World War II Army Air Force commander. Patton usually insisted that photographers only capture him in his "fighting face," but he is much more relaxed here with the war over. (NARA)

A LIFE IN WORDS

Patton died before he had a chance to write a complete autobiography. His wartime diary and the records of the Third Army were used to compile *War as I Knew It*, which appeared after his death in 1947. The first history of Patton's command in World War II *Patton and His Third Army* was written by his G-3 Liaison officer, Colonel Brenton Wallace, and it was published in 1946. Wallace was too close to Patton to offer a balanced historical perspective, but it remains an interesting first-hand account from the perspective of his staff. Another staffer's view of Patton was published in 1947, *Lucky Forward* by Robert S. Allen, a Washington journalist who had been on Patton's staff during the war. Patton's aide-de-camp, Colonel Charles Codman, was the author of *Drive*, a collection of letters back home to his wife which offers a witty, personal and affectionate look at the war from one of Patton's close confidantes. Patton's intelligence chief, Oscar Koch, wrote a brief account of his experiences that was not published until recently; since it was written shortly after the war, it skirted the issue of Ultra intelligence and the role it played in Patton's decisions.

Patton was very fond of recording his exploits, and both the Seventh Army and the Third Army prepared extravagant command histories after their campaigns, far more lavish than any comparable US unit. These are not well known as they were printed in a massive folio format that makes commercial reprints extremely difficult. The Third Army after-action-report was not declassified until 1981, which also has limited its circulation.

The Patton family was slow to make his diaries and papers public, and the first full-length biography to take advantage of access was Ladislas Farago's 1963 *Patton: Ordeal and Triumph*. Farago was a journalist and screenwriter

Patton's violent, vulgar, and inspirational speeches to his troops became the stuff of legend. They eventually emerged as an American cinematic icon with the release of the film *Patton* where they were depicted in the opening scene. Here he is seen addressing troops of the 82nd Airborne Division at Oujda, Morocco, prior to Operation *Husky* in June 1943. (NARA)

and he later wrote *The Last Days of Patton* challenging the zany conspiracy theories surrounding the general's death. Farago's biography remains a good read, but its importance lies in its role in the creation of the film *Patton*.

Frank McCarty, a VMI graduate and aide to General George Marshall during the war, had approached the Patton family about producing a film biography as early as 1953. He was rebuffed by the family, but 20th Century Fox bought the film rights both to Farago's biography and to Omar Bradley's memoirs. The film version was directed by Franklin Schaffner, a successful TV and movie director, and one of the screenwriters was Francis Ford Coppola who would go on to become a prominent director himself. Omar Bradley served as an advisor on the film, which helps account for his sympathetic portrayal by Karl Malden as well as the strongly anti-British and anti-Montgomery tone of the film. The Patton-Montgomery rivalry on Sicily portrayed in the film is a closer reflection of Bradley's perspective than Patton's. Although the lead role was offered to Burt Lancaster, he turned it down. This was fortunate in view of the stunning performance by George C. Scott, reinforced by Scott's closer physical resemblance to the general. The one forgivable discrepancy in Scott's performance was his gravelly voice, which was completely unlike Patton's own high-pitched voice. The film was released in 1970 and was an immediate critical and commercial success, winning seven Academy Awards including Best Picture. It is widely regarded as a classic American film and in 2003 was selected for preservation by the Library of Congress. This film, far more than any book, has cemented the Patton legend in American popular culture. Like any Hollywood effort, the film can be criticized for scores of minor historical inaccuracies and the inevitable distortions when condensing so vast a subject into so short a depiction. Yet *Patton* remains one of the best World War II films, and a rare example of a successful military film biography.

The movie only reinforced popular interest in Patton, and numerous books ensued. The family released Patton's papers to the Library of Congress in 1964, and the noted Army historian Martin Blumenson published a multi-volume collection of excerpts in 1972 as *The Patton Papers*. He later wrote one of the best short biographies of Patton which appeared in 1985. The outstanding biography of Patton to date is Carlo D'Este's *Patton: A Genius for War* which appeared in 1995. Colonel D'Este had already touched on Patton's World War II career in his several superb campaign histories, and his experience as a military historian helped add considerable depth and understanding to the biography. D'Este illuminated several controversies around Patton, and made a strong case that the rivalry between Patton and Montgomery had been exaggerated while at the same time the difficulties between Patton and Bradley, particularly in early 1944, had been swept under the rug. A far more negative biography of Patton appeared in 2002 by Professor Stanley Hirshson. Dennis Showalter has provided a splendid rumination on Patton and Rommel in his recent book that provides an insightful comparison between two archetypal American and German commanders.

FURTHER READING

Besides the several full-length biographies, many shorter biographies have also appeared over the years, often as a part of a series. The bibliography here is by no means exhaustive; the US Army Military History Institute index lists over 100 books with Patton in the title. Numerous specialized monographs dealing with aspects of Patton's campaigns have also been published, and a few are listed here. Another popular avenue of Patton-worship has been a number of books based on Patton's colorful quotes and aphorisms, how-to books for budding managers needing some martial inspiration for their bureaucratic battles.

Government reports

After-Action Report, Third US Army, 1 August 1944–9 May 1945 (2 volumes, 1945)

Report of Operations of the United States Seventh Army in the Sicilian Campaign, 10 July–17 August 1943 (1943)

XII Corps: Spearhead of Patton's Army (1945)

Saga of the XX "Ghost" Corps: Thru Hell and Highwater (1946)

Books

Allen, Robert S., *Lucky Forward, the History of Patton's Third Army* Vanguard: New York, 1947

Baron, Richard, *Raid! The Untold Story of Patton's Secret Mission* G. P. Putnam: New York, 1981

Blumenson, Martin, *Patton: The Man behind the Legend 1885–1945* William Morrow: New York, 1985

——, *The Patton Papers (1885–1940, 2 vol.; 1940–45, 1 vol.)* Houghton Mifflin: Boston, MA, 1972

Codman, Charles, *Drive* Little, Brown: New York, 1957

D'Este, Carlo, *Patton: A Genius for War* HarperCollins: New York, 1995

English, John, *Patton's Peers: the Forgotten Allied Field Army Commanders of the Western Front 1944–45* Stackpole: Mechanicsburg, PA, 2009

Essame, H., *Patton: A Study in Command* Charles Scribner's: New York, 1974

Farago, Ladislas, *Patton: Ordeal and Triumph* Obolensky: New York, 1964

——, *The Last Days of Patton* McGraw-Hill: New York, 1985

Hirshson, Stanley, *General Patton: A Soldier's Life* HarperCollins: New York, 2002

Hymel, Kevin, *Patton's Photographs: War as he saw it* Potomac: Dulles, VA, 2006

Koch, Oscar, *G-2: Intelligence for Patton* Schiffer: Atglen, PA, 1999

Lande, D. A., *I Was with Patton: First Person Accounts of WWII in George Patton's Command* MBI: Minneapolis, WI, 2002

Morelock, J. D., *Generals of the Ardennes: American Leadership in the Battle of the Bulge* National Defense University: Washington, DC, 1994

Patton Jr, George S., *War As I Knew It* Houghton Mifflin: New York, 1947

Phillips, Henry, *The Making of a Professional: Manton Eddy USA* Greenwood: Westport, CT, 2000

Prefer, Nathan, *Patton's Ghost Corps: Cracking the Siegfried Line* Presidio: New York, 1998

Price, Frank, *Troy Middleton: A Biography* LSU Press: Baton Rouge, LA, 1974

Province, Charles, *Patton's Third Army: A chronology of the Third Army Advance August 1944 to May 1945* Hippocrene: New York, 1992

——, *The Unknown Patton* Hippocrene: New York, 1983

Rickard, John, *Patton at Bay: The Lorraine Campaign, September to December 1944*(Praeger: Wesport, CT, 1999

Rodgers, Russ, *Historic Photos of General George Patton* Turner: Nashvile, TN, 2007

Showalter, Dennis, *Patton and Rommel: Men of war in the twentieth century* Berkley: New York, 2005

Spires, David, *Air Power for Patton's Army: The XIX TAC in the Second World War* GPO: Washington, DC, 2002

Wallace, Brenton, *Patton & His Third Army* Military Service Press: 1946

Winton, Harold, *Corps Commanders of the Bulge: Six American Generals and Victory in the Ardennes* University Press of Kansas: Lawrence, KS, 2007

GLOSSARY

AK	*Armeekorps*, abbreviation for a German corps
AOK	*Armeeoberkommando* (Army high command), frequently used as an abbreviation for a German field army
Army	A field army consisting of several corps, plus attached units including separate tank and tank destroyer battalions, field artillery battalions, engineer and support units.
Army group	The largest Allied tactical army formation, consisting of several armies
Corps	A tactical formation consisting of several divisions plus attached units such as separate field artillery battalions, engineer and support units.
ETO	European Theater of Operations, refers primarily to the campaigns of 1944–45 in north-west Europe, exclusive of the Mediterranean theater (MTO) or North African theater (NATO)
G-1	A US headquarters' personnel section responsible for the unit's administration as well as issues dealing with civilians and prisoners-of-war.
G-2	A US headquarters' intelligence section
G-3	A US headquarters' operations and training section
G-4	A US headquarters' logistics lection
TAC	US Army Air Force Tactical Air Command
VMI	Virginia Military Institute

INDEX